Precious Dreams and Living Nightmares:

a personal journey into grief

Kevin Burke

*For Sue –
A fellow traveller on
an unwelcome road –
with love
Kevin*

© 2025 Kevin Burke

All rights reserved, including the right to reproduce this book, or portions thereof, in any form without permission of the copyright owner.

The right of Kevin Burke to be identified as the author of this work has been asserted in accordance with the Copyright, Designs and Patents Act 1988

Cover image designed using Microsoft Designer Image Creator

First published February 2025

Dedicated to the love of my life, who is no more

When Winter comes, and singing ends; when darkness falls at last;
When broken is the barren bough, and light and labour past;
I'll look for thee, and wait for thee, until we meet again:
Together we will take the road beneath the bitter rain!
Together we will take the road that leads into the West,
And far away will find a land where both our hearts may rest.

J.R.R. Tolkien
The Lord of the Rings: The Two Towers

Table of Contents

Introduction 1

Chapter One: And this is where it starts 4

Chapter Two: The first few months..7

Chapter Three: Lonely in a crowd..11

Chapter Four: Why keep going?...13

Chapter Five: Inaction is the default....................................15

Chapter Six: Barney..18

Chapter Seven: The Black Hole..21

Chapter Eight: Barney walks 24

Chapter Nine: The cards come down....................................27

Chapter Ten: The first few seconds......................................30

Chapter Eleven: Treading water 32

Chapter Twelve: 19 weeks in ,.................................35

Chapter Thirteen: Sudoku weirdness....................................38

Chapter Fourteen: From caterpiller to butterfly................41

Chapter Fifteen: Roots & wings 45

Chapter Sixteen: The dream 47

Chapter Seventeen: The return..49

Chapter Eighteen: Six months 53
Chapter Nineteen: Facing The Future… the day after 55
Chapter Twenty: The voice in the morning 57
Chapter Twenty-One: Not just grief 59
Chapter Twenty-Two: Sobbing 61
Chapter Twenty-Three: A bad start 64
Chapter Twenty-Four: Robins 66
Chapter Twenty-Five: A milestone of sorts 69
Chapter Twenty- Six: Dreams 71
Chapter Twenty-Seven: Life expands 73
Chapter-Twenty-Eight: Triggers, triggers, triggers 76
Chapter Twenty-Nine: Stealth attack 79
Chapter Thirty: Nearly 9 months on and still a mess 81
Chapter Thirty-One: Bittersweet distractions 83
Chapter Thirty-Two: New Year malaise 86
Chapter Thirty-Three: Covid strikes! 88
Chapter Thirty-Four: A really tough day 91
Chapter Thirty-Five: Catharsis 93
Chapter Thirty-Six: Aftermath 96
Chapter Thirty-Seven: Turning a corner? 98
Chapter Thirty-Eight: Another little milestone 101
Chapter Thirty-Nine: Depression? 103
Chapter Forty: Another precious dream 106
Chapter Forty-One: Dusting 109
Chapter Forty-Two: A candle in the church 111

Chapter Forty-Three: The birthday 114

Chapter Forty-Four: Positivity 117

Chapter Forty-Five: A Mediterranean dream 120

Chapter Forty-Six: Another day, another bereavement course 123

Chapter Forty-Seven: A message from WhatsApp 125

Chapter Forty-Eight: Another meltdown 127

Chapter Forty-Nine: Easter Saturday 129

Chapter Fifty: A strange day – dreams, rain & counselling 133

Chapter Fifty-One: Triple whammy! 136

Chapter Fifty-Two: Ink 138

Chapter Fifty-Three: Looking forward 141

References and links 149

Acknowledgments 152

About the Author 154

Introduction
Or, perhaps, an explanation

On Easter day 2023, late in the evening, I lost my wife, my soulmate, my best friend, and the love of my life to suicide.

You will never know how difficult that sentence was for me to write, for I have hardly spoken about the circumstances of her death to anyone. The revelation will come as a shock to many of our family and friends, most of whom have, up to this point, assumed that she died as a result of the long illness that she had endured, an assumption I was happy not to challenge.

So before I begin, I want to take this opportunity to apologise to all who know us, and especially to our closest friends and family, for not having been honest with you from the beginning, and I hope that this book will go some way towards providing an explanation.

To lose a loved one is a terrible thing under any circumstances, but to lose a life partner in such a traumatic way – similar, I imagine, to losing someone through violence – is all but unbearable, and leaves scars that will never, *can* never heal.

It wasn't that I didn't *want* to tell people, it's just that in those early days I was simply incapable of speaking about what had happened. It was too raw, too terrible, too unfathomable. And that inability to talk about it led me into an unintended web of deceit that has imprisoned me ever since. It would be wrong to say that I lied to anyone – the chronic pain she endured, and the general deterioration in her health throughout those last few months absolutely contributed to her demise, so to that extent everything that I told people was true – but I always found ways to avoid going into the actual *details* of her death. So many times over the past year I have steeled myself to tell family and friends what happened, only to have my courage desert me at the last moment. Even now, as I sit here more than a year after the event, I find it difficult to put the horror of that night into words – and when I try, a tsunami of grief rises from somewhere deep within and chokes the breath from my lungs.

I also felt, rightly or wrongly, that the stigma still surrounding suicide would mean that people might think badly of her, and she didn't deserve that. Shirley was a kind, wonderful, vibrant person, but also intensely private, and would have hated to think that people were talking about her. Dying from a prolonged illness is tragic but comprehensible, often a blesséd relief, and a cause for sympathy. Suicide is a different kind of tragedy – one that is much harder to understand – and one which fuels gossip.

To some extent we are lucky. We are living at a time when mental health issues are rising to the top of the agenda, and the taboos that surround them are gradually being chipped away – but there is so much more to do. I never thought of Shirley as having mental health issues *per se* – not in the beginning at any rate – but as the months went by I witnessed her descent into depression and anxiety, fuelled by an increasing sense of hopelessness as she struggled to cope with the pain that assailed her moment by moment, day after day – a pain that the medical profession seemed at a loss to find a reason for, much less an effective way to treat – until finally reaching the stage where she had simply had enough, and could go on no longer.

This book does not seek to speak about, or attempt to explain, why this talented, funny, intelligent woman took the course of action that she did. Rather it is an examination of the first year of my own journey through grief, a year in which I have tried – and more often than not, failed – to cope with, and make sense of, what happened.

For no matter how much support we may have, no matter how much our friends and family may rally round, ultimately it is a journey that we have to take on our own: when we are alone with our thoughts; when we are confronted by a whiff of scent, or the snatch of a song; or any one of the myriad memories that are just too beautiful to bear.

And, perhaps most poignantly of all, when we close the bedroom door at the end of the day and lie in the cold, empty darkness, praying for sleep.

Yet what I *don't* want is for people to feel sorry for me – though I'm sure that many will – and I'm equally sure there will be those who will accuse me of wallowing in self-pity, and be wondering why I couldn't just pull myself together and get on with life – though I suspect such people wouldn't have picked up a book like this in the first place.

But if you have found this book because you too are grieving, then my hope is that some part of it may strike a chord with you – as parts of other books have with me – and provide some small scraps of comfort as you try to navigate your own way through this living nightmare that we call bereavement.

Chapter One
And this is where it starts…

I thought I understood grief, having dealt with the deaths of my grandparents, my parents, and two of my older siblings. But what happened on that Easter night last year catapulted me onto a whole other level of grieving… grief on steroids.

Statistically, death by suicide is horribly and tragically common, yet we think it inconceivable that it could touch our own family… until the awful moment that it does. After all, we are programmed for self-preservation, aren't we? Conditioned to survive at all costs. So it is incomprehensible that anyone should willingly take their life – certainly it was to me – and yet it happens, over and over again. And with each life lost, other lives are devastated. Lives of people who could see the signs but were at a loss as to how to help. Lives of people who were so far in denial that they failed to understand just how serious things had become. Lives of people who lived every day in the desperate hope that the situation would suddenly improve, that a corner would be turned, that there would be light at the end of the tunnel. In short, lives of people like me.

Then, suddenly, it has happened, that terrible thing that you never believed ever could. And there is nothing you can do but weep; weep uncontrollably for a life cut short, for all the things you could have said and done but didn't, and for all the things you said and did but wish you hadn't. Guilt and regret, your two inescapable companions as you take your first faltering steps into the unknown.

I blundered through those first couple of weeks in a haze, bundling the dog into the car and taking him some distance from home for his walks so there was no chance of bumping into anyone I knew – I simply couldn't face people at that stage. Yet in spite of myself, there were good friends who popped round to see how I was, never wanting to intrude, but often dropping off supplies, and offering a listening ear and a shoulder to cry on should I need it.

And there were times when I most definitely did.

There were things that had to be done, of course. Death brings with it a bewildering amount of administration, so those early days were full. But come the evenings I would simply sit, letting the darkness thicken around me, until it was time to take myself off to bed.

I thank God that throughout this process I have had no problem sleeping. It was one of the first questions my doctor asked me, obviously standing by with a prescription for sleeping pills or the like, which thankfully I was able to decline. Sleep has been my refuge, my escape from the terrible reality of my circumstances, and has remained so to this day.

But after a few months had passed, and I was casting about for anything that might help with the dreadful, debilitating grief that seized me during my waking hours, it was suggested that perhaps I should keep a diary, or a journal, of my thoughts and feelings – that perhaps the act of getting them down on paper might be beneficial to the healing process. I had already established that my brain no longer had the concentration necessary for meaningful typing on a keyboard, so I decided instead to record snippets of how I was feeling on the voice recorder of my phone, and though I didn't realise it at the time, that was where the seeds of this little book were sown.

What follows are the transcriptions of those recordings, along with a bit of commentary written with the hindsight afforded by listening to them again now, more than nine months after the first one was recorded.

I have deliberately transcribed them exactly as they were recorded, with no editing apart from cutting out the constant 'ums' and 'errs' which have been replaced for the most part by an ellipsis to preserve the halting, broken, and irregular flow of the originals. I wanted to retain the rawness, the honesty, and the immediacy of the pieces, so I present them to you in their rough, unpolished state – though of course what you will *not* hear are the many times I break down; the many times I dissolve into tears; the many times my voice cracks; or the raw emotion that underpins the bulk of the recordings. That you will have to imagine.

In effect what you hold in your hand is a time capsule – the thoughts, the feelings, and the pain I experienced throughout that first year of grief preserved, as it were, in aspic. By the time you read it, more time will have elapsed, and who knows where I will be along the rocky road of my bereavement journey. But what I do know is that nothing will be the same again, no matter how many years flow by, and that is the awful reality that somehow I need to come to terms with.

I hope with all my heart that writing this book will be part of that process.

Chapter Two
The first few months

As previously mentioned, I did not begin laying my thoughts down in this way until the best part of three months had gone by, so I feel that before we get to the transcriptions, I should quickly run through the main events of those lost months before the recordings begin.

Shirley did not want a funeral, her instructions were clear on that, opting instead for a direct cremation. I was determined to respect her wishes, though the awful reality of doing so meant that I could not be there with her at the end of her journey. Fortunately, the funeral director – a wonderfully kind and caring soul –understood my distress and suggested that I might like to be there first thing in the morning as they loaded her body into the van. I know this might sound grim, but like a starving dog at his master's table, I was happy to accept whatever crumb of comfort might be thrown to me.

Most importantly, it meant that I got to say goodbye, with as much love and decorum as the circumstances allowed, and for that I was profoundly grateful.

She was, however, happy for me to arrange a celebration of life service, a project I embraced with enthusiasm – though putting together a slideshow of her life was a fraught and lengthy experience, as I could only look at a handful of photos at a time before dissolving into tears and having to leave it for that day. Yet it is a testament to

Shirley that everyone I asked to play a role in the day agreed without hesitation, and I am so very grateful to each and every one of them. Once the day arrived, everything came together beautifully, and the service was a fitting tribute to the Shirley that I knew and loved, becoming a moment in time that will remain one of my most treasured memories.

Of the many aspects of my new situation that I discovered over those first few months, one of the most unexpected was that my grief-addled brain couldn't concentrate on anything for very long. So, as I was unable to read a novel or watch a film, my evenings became filled with box sets: half-hour comedies that didn't demand much attention. We had picked up a set of all eleven seasons of 'Frasier' on DVD – a bargain charity shop find – and during lockdown had enjoyed watching our way through all 264 episodes. We joked that if either of us succumbed to the virus, the other could watch them all through again, so that's where I began. Frasier kept me going through those awful early weeks, and I have a lot to thank him for.

I had, of course, cancelled all my work in those first weeks –a performer by trade, I hardly felt like being very entertaining back then – but one job remained in the diary: the Corfe Castle street party for the King's coronation. As the date grew closer, I began to think that perhaps I had made a mistake in thinking I could do the gig; that I wasn't ready; that it would prove too much. But it was only a couple of hours and local, so I packed the car and set off – and once there soon discovered that being at work was strangely beneficial. While I was working, I couldn't think of anything else, and so it has proved with all the jobs I have done since. What I do have to be careful of though, is not taking on too much. I find that my stress levels rise very quickly these days, so I need to give myself plenty of time between jobs to ensure that I can get all the preparation done well in advance. I need to feel totally on top of whatever I am booked to do, or my adrenaline levels go off the chart.

Then, as one month gave way to another, the turning of the page on the calendar brought an unwelcome jolt. For there, like a black cloud sweeping in from the sea, loomed the date of our wedding anniversary. What was I to do with it? Would I stay at home and descend into the Slough of Despond, or should I do something more positive? Whatever I decided, I knew that it would be a gut-wrenchingly awful day.

A few weeks earlier, I had waved a sad farewell to the car that Shirley and I had bought together some twelve years previously (it's truly staggering just how many memories a vehicle can hold) and purchased a camper from one of my neighbours. One of the many terrible things about sudden bereavement is that all your plans for the future are literally stopped dead. Friends will tell you that you should still do them, as a way of keeping your joint dreams alive, but that's easier said than done. Plans made for a loving couple aren't so easy to translate to a grieving singleton. But we had always intended to get a camper and explore those parts of the country that we had never visited, and when my neighbour mentioned in casual conversation that he had decided to get rid of his, I felt the hand of fate reaching out to me. This was something I actually *could* do, and my little dog Barney and I could take off on some adventures.

A left-hand drive American import, the van needed a decent trip so that I could acclimatise myself to a surprisingly different way of driving, and the opportunity presented itself when I received a certificate stating that some of our oldest friends had given a donation to the Woodland Trust[1] so that two trees could be dedicated to Shirley's memory. They were in a grove in Avon Valley Woods, Devon, so that's where I resolved to spend our wedding anniversary. I booked a nearby campsite, packed the van, bundled Barney inside, and set off.

Arriving at the campsite, I had what I can only describe as an anxiety attack – something I had never experienced before – and suddenly felt more alone than I had ever felt in my life, so much so that I began to doubt whether I had done the right thing. But my neighbours on the site were so lovely, as were the site owners, that I began to feel much better about the whole enterprise and come the next day, I spent our wedding anniversary weeping in the woods with Barney at my side, which somehow felt exactly the right thing to do.

Before we left the following day, while walking Barney alongside the stream that bounced and gurgled its way along the southern boundary of the campsite, I was moved to record a piece on my phone about how idyllic this part of the country was, and how much I longed for Shirley to be able to share it with me.

And that was how this project began.

Chapter Three
Lonely in a crowd

19th July 19:43

Thoughts on bereavement, number one.

If you say you are lonely, people will rally round… say "come for a meal," "come out for a walk with us," "drop in and have a cup of tea anytime," which is all lovely, and much appreciated… and yes, it helps. But the truth is, you're only lonely for one person… you're lonely for the one company that you cannot have… the one person that you'll never have in your life again. And that's the tragedy.

*

When I recorded this, the memory of my trip to Devon was still very strong in my mind – my first trip away on my own (apart from the dog, of course, who was a godsend – I don't know how I'd have survived that trip without him), bringing with it the inescapable truth that this is what it is going to be like from now on. This is the new, unwanted reality of my life – and it sucks.

A former colleague of Shirley's who came to her celebration service, and who had lost her husband to cancer a couple of years previously, warned me that for the first few months people would be wonderful – rallying round, supportive and sympathetic – but that after a while that support would drop away, as people began to assume that you were 'over it', and were moving on with your life. I have to say that so far that has not been my experience. It is true that I have become aware of people treating me as though I am getting along okay, but on the whole, the people who were my rocks at the beginning have remained so to this day, and for that I am eternally grateful.

To be fair, it's my own fault that people regard me as doing well and getting back to normal, because when they ask, I invariably say: "Oh, you know, up and down" or, even worse, "I'm alright… you know, keeping going." So during the summer I decided that I would write a blog post to tell people exactly how I was feeling.[2] The day after I shared it on social media, I bumped into a friend who sidled up to me and exclaimed, somewhat sheepishly: "Oh my goodness, I daren't ask how you are!" which seemed to indicate that the post had had the desired effect.

I did have one person – not someone I know particularly well, but who I bumped into at an event over Christmas – who asked me how I was, and when I told him I was still grieving and wasn't coping particularly well, answered: "Still??" To be fair to him, he quickly qualified his comment by saying that he couldn't imagine what it must be like, having never been in that position, but his initial reaction serves to illustrate that sympathy often has a shelf-life.

Chapter Four
Why keep going?

20th July 07:53

Thoughts on bereavement, two.

There is no real choice other than to keep going, but to keep going to where, or for what purpose, is a complete mystery.

*

From the first, I knew that if I was to make it through the months that lay ahead, I couldn't think in terms of the great swathes of meaningless time that stretched before me like the cold, unforgiving Arctic tundra – but needed instead to take one moment at a time, just getting through the days by simply putting one foot in front of the other. Any thoughts of the future, any plans I might have had, or ambitions I might have hoped for had ceased to exist from the moment the police knocked at my door in the early hours of that Easter Monday. All I had left was the plodding of my feet from one minute to the next, inexorably shuffling forward in the darkness.

A good friend of mine, a retired vicar as it happens, who has been a rock of support throughout this terrible time, said that bereavement is like being forced onto a train that you don't want to be on. You don't know where it's going, and there's no way you can get off. I don't think that's a bad analogy, so long as you can also visualise the stark terror that such a situation brings with it, as you uselessly claw at the locked doors, desperately searching for a way out.

Of course, as the months go by, there are times when you become numb to the awfulness of your situation and, lulled by the constant rhythm of the train into a kind of torpor, simply allow yourself to be carried along – sitting motionless in the carriage, passively accepting whatever fate awaits you down the line. And now, a year later, that's pretty much where I am – just being carried along, day after day after day – and that it could ever be any different feels like an impossibility.

Another friend described it as the most miserable club you never wanted to be a member of.

And that's true too.

Chapter Five
Inaction is the default

20th July 08:59

Thoughts on bereavement, number three.

Inaction is the order of the day. I could quite easily stay in bed and do nothing. When I'm up, I could quite easily sit in the chair all day… and do nothing. Even a simple thing like turning on the television requires a huge act of will. Concentration… concentration is almost non-existent. Everything has to be forced. There is no enthusiasm, no reason for doing anything, All the things I used to enjoy doing have turned to dust. I force myself… I force myself continually. I make lists… tick them off… of things I need to do, but the need is simply to get through from getting up in the morning to going back to bed at night. That time has to be filled.

*

By this stage, most of the legal and administrative tasks had been completed, including the redrafting of my own will, and the time-consuming business of putting together my statement and evidential material for the coroner. This was for use at the inquest, which had been opened then immediately adjourned – the normal way of things, apparently – with a provisional date for the actual hearing booked for the twelfth of November, a wait of some eight months which I was told was due to a backlog of cases – a hangover from the Covid years, I suspect. I duly wrote the date onto the wall calendar and circled it – another dark cloud lurking in the far reaches of my consciousness, drawing ever closer and more menacing as the days ticked by.

The need for distraction, for something – anything – to fill the void of my days became a priority. I began taking on a small amount of work, just what I felt I could cope with and no more, and the associated preparation gave me a focus. Of course, my regular couple of dog-walks a day were providing a great deal of solace, though there were days when that might expand to three, or even four. I had got used to grabbing Barney's lead and hollering "Walkies!" whenever I felt the grief closing in, so we both got plenty of exercise during those days – and still do.

It was out of this need for distraction that I made a momentous decision. I would book tickets for the Cropredy Festival[3]. This was far more significant than you might think, as Cropredy was very dear to us both and, until Covid struck – followed by Shirley's illness – was a regular feature of our year. But this was exactly the sort of thing I had envisaged Barney and I getting up to in the van, and as I had lived in hope (as I always did) that this year Shirley would feel up to going, it had already been in my mind that this might be the year we would return. Except that now, that 'we' would be just me and the dog.

I managed to ascertain from a quick Facebook post that there would be people there that I knew, and the preparation for three days camping in the van consumed a great deal of my time. The festival itself is in August, and as the date grew closer, I found myself wondering – once again – whether I had made a monumental mistake.

Despite my misgivings, we set off in hopeful excitement, but as I arrived and turned into the field which would be our home for the next few days, I caught sight of the stage and stalls, festooned with myriad multi-coloured flags and all the associated trappings of a music festival, and burst into tears. The memories simply overwhelmed me.

But someone, somewhere was smiling down on me that day, for I found myself camped next to a chap who was similarly on his own, and who had also been widowed in the last couple of years. We formed a connection and found we could speak fondly together of our wives and share our experiences of trying to find a way through, which was an absolute godsend.

Another striking coincidence of that first day was that in the crush of people waiting for the festival field to open, I found myself standing right next to one of the friends who I had said I would look out for, never dreaming they would be quite so easy to find. Whether this was by happy accident or by Divine intervention it's impossible to tell, but it's strange the way things work out sometimes.

In the end, I have to admit that it was a genuinely lovely experience – by far the nicest time I had spent since Shirley passed away. Poignant, yes, and I shed many a tear throughout the course of the festival, but in hindsight I can hardly believe that I was considering not going. It really was food for the soul.

And I'm pretty sure Barney enjoyed himself too.

Chapter Six
Barney

20th July 09:11

Thoughts on bereavement, number four.

As I record this, you may be able to hear Barney barking in the background. Were it not for that little dog, I would not have got through to this point. He gives me a focus, something to get up for, something to look after… and in return he gives me love and affection and makes the house far less empty than it would otherwise be. A dog is such a positive thing.

*

Once the police had left – I think it was round about 3.30 am, though I can't remember the exact time – Barney and I went to bed. It was the one and only time he's slept on the bed with me – usually he sleeps in his crate – but I couldn't go to bed alone. Not that night.

Amazingly, I slept until my phone woke me at about 7.30. I had sent an urgent, crazed text to my son just before I went through to the bedroom, a text he received when he awoke, and rang me immediately. After an emotional phone call, he made the necessary arrangements at work, came straight down, and stayed a couple of days. I can't tell you how wonderful it was to have him here, and I was so grateful that he could make the time. It meant everything to me.

.While I awaited his arrival, I had to take Barney for a walk – a necessary habit that has continued, day after day, month after month. No matter how I may be feeling, no matter how low and desperate, no matter what may have happened in my day, Barney has to be exercised, has to be fed, has to be looked after – and as I said in the recording, in return he gives me unwavering love and support. He is a sensitive soul and has been there for me every step of the way, as I have been for him – and as I have promised I always will be.

A long-haired miniature dachshund, Barney is, like all dogs, a creature of habit and routine, with an extraordinarily accurate internal clock. When Shirley was working, she would come home for lunch every day, and five minutes or so before she could be seen walking up the road, Barney would take his place in the window to watch out for her. There was no prompting from me, he just knew what the time was.

And it goes without saying that if the clock slips even one minute beyond five o'clock and I haven't put his dinner down yet, the looks I get would make St Francis feel inadequate.

One of his little morning routines, after I had let him out of his crate and he'd visited the back garden for a wee, was to potter through to the bedroom to see Shirley, who would still be in bed, waiting for me to bring through cups of tea. And for weeks after she died, Barney repeated that behaviour, unable to fathom why she wasn't there. He would also seek out those places in the house where her smell was strongest, and would sit there for hours, obviously missing her as much as I was. He became quite listless, in fact, and was obviously depressed. He appeared to have lost his zest for life, and I knew exactly how he felt.

Together we have grieved, and together we have had to find ways to come to terms with our new reality. A reality that neither of us would have chosen or wanted. One result of this is that he has become far more clingy than he used to be (as I write this, he is curled up on my lap) but I can understand that – because so have I.

There is an internet meme which runs something along the lines of: 'When I reached for a hand, I found a paw.' Schmaltzy, perhaps, but in my case, never a truer word was spoken.

I have taken his paw, and together we have boarded the train. We may have no idea where we are going, but at least we are travelling together.

Chapter Seven
The Black Hole

20th July 09:17

Thoughts on bereavement, number five.

It has been fourteen weeks now since Shirley died, and people tell me how well I'm doing. I don't know how they can tell: I put a face on for other people. There is hardly anyone who knows what I'm really going through. Even I cannot tell how well I'm doing because there is no yardstick. Everyone's grief is so different. Everyone reacts in so many different ways, and yet there are common factors throughout the grieving process. The truth is, there is a huge hole – a black hole – in the centre of my life which is sucking my life into it. Everything I used to do, everything I used to know, everything I used to be is sucked into that black hole, and at the moment it feels like they will never return. I stand on the edge of that huge black hole and stare into the abyss. And though I may put on a smile, and a face – a mask for those who speak to me and who I speak to – the truth is, I am an actor, a good actor… I know how to put it on, I know how to play a role. I know how to be what they expect me to be.

But in truth, there is just the hole.

*

This recording formed the main body of the blog that I referred to in chapter three and accurately reflects the yawning gulf that I feel between how I am – or seem to be – when I am in the company of others, and how I am when at home alone. I can also appreciate why people are constantly encouraging me *not* to be alone. But as I also said in that same chapter, you are pining for the company of that one person that you can no longer have, and nothing else will ever come close – nothing and no one can fill that void.

I have given a lot of thought to why I am so adept at putting on a mask in front of others, of appearing to be something that I'm not. Certainly, there is much that comes from my chosen profession – as an entertainer you need to be able to hide whatever is going on in your personal life and be, as I often describe it, 'professionally jolly.' You are part of everyone else's good time, and you can't destroy that by letting your personal feelings come to the fore. If you did, you wouldn't last long in the business.

This gives rise, of course, to such common tropes as the 'tears of a clown' and 'smile, though your heart is breaking.' After all, the show must go on.

But there is more to it than that.

I was twelve when my dad died and was immediately thrust into the role of 'man of the house'. Very much a mark of the parenting style of that generation, I had been brought up to believe in the 'stiff upper lip' – that it was weak to show emotion – and for a nervous, highly-strung, sensitive young boy this was not the best thing to have hammered into you. This was a time when if tears did break through you would be labelled a 'cry-baby,' and it was common for my parents to employ the not-so-veiled threat of 'stop crying or I'll give you something to cry about.' Moreover, it was a time when the common perception was that crying was something that only girls did – In public at any rate – and that I and many boys like me had to be a 'brave little soldier.' So it is hardly surprising that I became skilled at 'putting on a brave face,' or that so many of my generation have grown up to be emotionally repressed.

But while I still see pockets of what I believe is now referred to as toxic masculinity, and still witness sensitive young boys being told to 'man up,' I thank God that on the whole things have changed, and mostly for the better. For to say that the lad I was back then would have been unable to cope with this unrelenting pressure of grief would be an understatement.

Chapter Eight
Barney walks

21st July 11:02

Thoughts on bereavement, number seven.

Amongst the many changes of behaviour of my little dog Barney since Shirley passed away, perhaps the most notable is this: when Shirley was ill, and always at home, it was very difficult for me to get Barney out. I would have to drag him along for a walk. But as soon as he realised we had turned round and were on our way home again, he would literally run to get back to Shirley. Since she's passed away, absolutely the opposite happens. He can't wait to get out, and so long as we are moving away from the house he will dash along at a rate of knots. As soon as we turn and he knows he's on his way back, I have to drag him almost all the way. It's almost as though he realises there's nothing left for him at home – a sentiment with which I absolutely agree.

*

Eagle-eyed readers will have noticed that this is not, in fact, '*Thoughts on bereavement, number seven*', but actually number six, the fact that I misnumbered the recording being an indication of my general mental state at that time. My grief-addled brain was all over the place.

But it was not only my own mental health that I was trying to look after, but Barney's too, and there is no question that our daily walks were hugely beneficial for us both. I have mentioned before that he was showing all the signs of depression, and I had read that sniffing was a great stress reliever in dogs, helping with anxiety and generally boosting their well-being. So as much as I might want to get up a head of steam and forge ahead at a healthy pace, I suppressed that instinct to allow Barney the freedom to stop and sniff to his heart's content. And I guess that the (sometimes frustratingly) slower pace I was forced to adopt was good for me too, for it meant that I noticed and appreciated more of my surroundings, as we gently wended our way along the highways and byways, one sniff at a time.

At home I made an effort to ensure that he knew he was loved and cherished, played with him as much as time would allow – though I suspect that the games he and I share together are no substitute for the fun he used to have when there were two of us to play with – and did my best to serve his meals (and regular snacks) on time. In short, like any single parent, I indulged him in a pitiful attempt to make up for the missing adult in his life.

I also took the decision not to use the word 'mummy' when I spoke to him, as he knew this word well and would immediately go looking for her – a strategy which helped me too, as to do so simply tore me apart.

Another consequence of this new 'single parent' status is that I have to make arrangements for Barney whenever I need to go to work, or anywhere else that he can't come. I have been wonderfully fortunate on that score, in that I have good friends who love him as much as I do and are always happy to have him when they can. But I continually worry about what I would do if they couldn't, for whatever reason. There has only been one hiccup so far, and on that occasion, I had no choice but to take him with me and leave him in the van while I did my job, but that is far from ideal and would be impossible in the heat of summer when the inside of any vehicle becomes like an oven. Such thoughts just add to my overall anxieties concerning Barney, along with: what if he hurt himself? became ill? got out and couldn't be found? or, heaven forbid, was stolen?

I recorded the following as a coda to the piece entitled 'Barney' on the twentieth of July and originally put it at the end of chapter five to keep the recordings in sequence, but on reflection it seems to fit much better here.

I love him so much… and yet I am desperately afraid that something will happen to him, so I am over-protective. In truth, I was always protective towards him but now that has risen exponentially. If I were to lose him as well, I literally do not know how I could go forward.

And that about sums it up.

Chapter Nine
The cards come down

23rd July 15:32

So yesterday was a difficult day. I made the decision to take down all of the condolence cards which have after all been up for three months now, and it was tough. Not only the physical act of taking them down, but also as I read the comments in each one, I was unfortunately… yeah… not so good. And now the room looks very like it does after you've taken the Christmas decorations down, and it looks very bare, until you get used to what it actually looks like without all the extras. Of course, the cards will stay with me for always. I'm not getting rid of a single one of them.

*

I received fifty-six cards, along with another thirty-four condolence messages by letter, Facebook, or email. At her celebration service I had provided a book for people to write their thoughts and memories of Shirley, and after the event I transcribed all the email messages into the book alongside those from the service. Literally a labour of love, and just one of the tasks that made me feel a little better, as I felt I was doing it for Shirley.

Writing this now, though, I can't help but think of the imagery of a house of cards – that no matter how carefully you may build it, you can never know when it will all suddenly come tumbling down.

Shirley and I had originally got together in the early 1980's, when we were both in our twenties, and although we talked of marriage then, I was young and stupid and let her go, a decision which devastated her at the time, and set us both on the path to less than happy marriages with other people. When we found each other again some thirty years later, it was as though the intervening years had never existed. Both once again single and, at least in my case, hoping that age and experience had brought with it a modicum of wisdom, I pledged that this time we would be together longer than we had been apart. It was a vow that I was convinced I could keep.

In the event, we had thirteen wonderful years together. I know the phrase 'never a cross word' is a bit of a cliché, but in our case, it was utterly true. We just got on together, loved being in each other's company. By whatever definition you might wish to apply we were soulmates, pure and simple – and loved each other totally and absolutely.

All of which made her descent into a maelstrom of pain, both physical and mental, so very hard to bear. I believe that she mourned for the life we had had together, a life that she thought she would never get back. And as the months passed and her pain grew worse, so the frustration of the situation led to our becoming tetchy with each other for the first time in all our years together.

Everyone who loses a loved one feels guilt at what they wished they had done and said, and what they wished they had *not* done and said. The 'what if's' and the 'would've, could've, should'ves' are the things that haunt us most.

In his book 'The Madness of Cricf,'[4] Rovorond Richard Coles says:

"I feel in that moment, full force, that I should have been kinder, loved him more strongly, made him happier. I could have done, but I did not, because I was too self-absorbed, and there is nothing I can do about it now."

I used to tell Shirley that regrets are pointless, because you can't change the past, but instead should look towards the future, and work to make that the best that it can be.

Well, now that sentiment feels hollow and meaningless, and my regrets are as countless as the stars in the sky – and just as immutable.

Chapter Ten
The first few seconds

23rd July 15:33

Bereavement thoughts whatever the hell this is… I don't even think I numbered the last one.

Anyway, this is just a little aside about a phenomenon that I am experiencing but which apparently is not uncommon. And that is that in the first few seconds as you wake in the morning you can still… you are still aware that the other person is there. But of course they aren't, and that comes home to you very quickly… like I say, after a couple seconds. But for those first couple of seconds, it is a bizarre, bizarre moment. I guess eventually it will wear off… I guess.

*

Brushing your hand across the empty pillow; turning over onto the cold, unslept-in side of the bed; the absence of the other person's breathing; the slow opening of your eyes onto an uninhabited side of the bedroom – these are the things that bring you back to the harsh reality of your situation, to the unpalatable truth of your loneliness. It is said that every time this happens, you are bereaved all over again, as you realise that you are alone, and that you will still be alone tomorrow, and tomorrow, and tomorrow – as Shakespeare so eloquently put it[5]. And finding yourself alone in a place once so bound up with the intimacy of couplehood is an unfathomable cruelty.

Writing this now, almost a year after I made the recording, I'm afraid I have to say that the feeling of not being alone when I first awake is still with me. It only lasts a second or two, but it's still there, and I wonder whether it will ever leave me.

I have washed the bedding many times since Shirley passed away and each time, I have carefully replaced her folded nightie between the pillows where it always belonged – and belongs still. I look across at her side of the bedroom, to where her dressing gown still hangs on the side of the wardrobe and her fleece jacket – an early Christmas present and hardly worn – hangs on a hanger from the wardrobe door. Apart from the emotional wrench of letting them go, which I am still not in the right frame of mind to do, the room would feel crushingly empty without them. So her possessions still sit, stand or hang where they always have.

During the early summer I sat outside in the garden reading, and found I needed a bookmark. I knew that there was one in the last book Shirley was reading, a book that was still where she had left it on her bedside table, so I walked through to get it. But when I got to the book, I couldn't bring myself to take the bookmark out. Utterly illogical, because I knew she wouldn't be coming back to finish it, and yet there I stood, in floods of tears, unable to extract the bookmark, and having to resort to a scrap of paper instead.

Ridiculous, I know, but if I can't even manage to remove a bookmark, how on earth am I going to be able to clear her drawers or her wardrobe?

Chapter Eleven
Treading water

31st July 11.42

It is sixteen weeks to the day since I lost my beautiful Shirley, and I've already had a weep this morning. In truth, there has not been a day in those sixteen weeks when I have not cried at some point or another... most days several times during the day. All I can say is I am not weeping uncontrollably anymore. Not weeping as though I felt I would never stop, as I was during the first few weeks, so I guess that is progress and some would say I was getting better – ha! – whatever that might mean. I'm sitting here, cuddling the dog, with a huge jobs list that I've made for myself so that I can get through my day, filling the time from waking up to going to bed. As I've said before, none of that, none of it I have any enthusiasm for, no motivation for doing it... and today motivation seems to be particularly lacking. So I'm sitting here with the dog, doing nothing but recording this thought. Gosh, I'm just treading water in life... just treading, treading water to try and keep my head above the waves.

*

Motivation remains a constant battle. The urge to do nothing is strong, and unless I have something that I *need* to do, that urge will often win out. Hence the interminable jobs lists that I create. I am always thankful when I get to the end of the day and I can retreat into bed and sleep... sleep being my only escape from the all-pervading awfulness that infects my soul. But I am also thankful when I have managed to achieve *something* during the day, no matter how small. Sometimes that amounts to little more than walking the dog and making food, though now there is a new imperative, in that I am trying to write this book, and that gives me a focus for an hour or two. It should be said that I can't bring myself to write every day, so this is taking far longer than it might have done, but it is a step in the right direction. And perhaps, once I've finally got this finished, it might prove a catalyst for me to get back to writing fiction. That's my hope, at any rate.

Having mentioned food in that last paragraph, I feel the need to confess that I am, and have always been, a comfort eater. When I'm feeling low it is most often the fridge or the cupboard that I turn to, so I try not to have too many treats in the house, though to be honest, you might as well define a treat as *anything* tasty that I can munch away at. Naturally, this has the unwelcome side-effect of adding to my weight, and that's a constant battle. Thank goodness for the dog walks, which burn off calories and therefore redress the balance a bit.

Cooking was always my thing – the closest I've ever come to having a hobby, I suppose – and even before Shirley became ill, I would make most of our meals. I always found it therapeutic, and after a difficult or stressful day I could always relax by strapping on the apron and creating something delicious. I still cook, of course, but have lost the joy that I used to find in it. Now I prepare food because I need to eat, rather than because I enjoy doing it. But at least I haven't succumbed to the dreaded 'ready meals.' Not yet, at any rate.

My go-to cookery books are anything written by Nigel Slater or the Hairy Bikers, the latter being responsible – under their guise as the Hairy *Dieters* – for my discovering truly tasty, calorie-controlled recipes which have been fundamental in helping me lose weight, so I am forever in their debt.

A short while before I began to write this book, I heard the sad news that Dave Myers, one of the eponymous bikers, had died. And though I had never met him, I wept as though I had lost a friend.

Chapter Twelve
19 weeks in

23rd August 09:17

So it's now been about, well a little over 19 weeks since I lost Shirley... and I haven't recorded any of these for a few weeks. Don't know whether that means that I've just been too busy – because I keep myself busy constantly because it's the only way I seem to be able to get through – or whether my mental health's improving. I don't know. But anyway... the... what I wanted to say today was that... was that the... the crippling grief is still there, and still comes in huge waves that pretty much destroy me but not as, not probably as... as regularly as they used to. Although it is still true that there's still not been a day when I haven't cried at some point. I'm sure that day will come, but I don't know when... or if. Instead, I've sort of dropped into a kind of numbness, I suppose. I still have no enthusiasm for anything, no real interest in anything although I have managed to... to watch TV quite a lot and... and found some interest in that, but still can't read, still haven't written anything, still feels like I'm just in a treading water scenario, except that treading water even is a... is an activity which needs energy, and at the moment I feel like my energy is completely lacking. I am, as I said, just numb. Just... just numb.

*

Listening to this recording now, it is obvious that there is a central theme to many of these pieces – that of apathy, lack of interest, lack of motivation, lack of *joy* – and I'm sorry to report that this hasn't really changed, though I am aware that some things have, very slowly, improved over the last year. I no longer weep uncontrollably, and I can concentrate much better, to the end that I can watch a film, read a novel, or, as this book proves, write again.

Grief still hits like a jackhammer at times, though. C.S. Lewis, in his book 'A Grief Observed,'[6] describes grief like a circling bomber – you know it's there; you can hear it circling, but you never know when it will drop its bombs. A comparison which strongly chimed with me when I first read it.

There are, to be fair, a bewildering number of ways to think about grief, probably as many as there are people who grieve, and not all of them are going to speak to you. Everyone's grief is different, and everyone copes in a different way – a way that is specific and personal to their own circumstances – which means that often, what people will tell you can feel crass and patronising. Any grief counsellor worth their salt will acknowledge that, and though they will inevitably form connections and draw comparisons with established models, at the end of the day you can only do what you feel is right for you.

As an example, I submit the much vaunted 'five stages of grief' (also known as the Kubler-Ross model[7]) as exhibit 'A.' I'm sure most will be familiar with this, the supposed five stages that you pass through as you navigate your own grief 'journey,' that is: Denial, Anger, Bargaining, Depression, and Acceptance. I'm not saying this isn't a useful model, but it certainly isn't a linear journey through the stages, and many won't experience all five. In my own case there has as yet been only a profound sense of loss and sadness – the depression bit of the model, I suppose. There was never any denial, because I knew she had gone from the moment the police received the official time of death over the radio, as they sat on my sofa on that fateful night. And seeing her laid out in the funeral director's parlour only served to reinforce that certainty. She had gone, and there was no way back from that.

Nor have I felt any anger, because I understood the amount of pain she was experiencing, understood the hopelessness that she felt, and knew all too well that she'd had enough. So no, I could never feel angry at her for what she did. Anger at the doctors? Anger at God? Anger at myself? Perhaps I should have, and I'm sure there are many that would, but I have felt none of these things. I suppose there is a possibility that I may in the future, but not now, not at any time throughout this wretched year.

Bargaining, likewise. Of course I would give anything to have her back, but I know that could never happen, so what point would there be in bargaining? And with whom would I bargain? Once again, in the C.S. Lewis book, he speaks about the essential selfishness of wanting his wife back, when that would only mean that she would have to endure death all over again. One of the most heartbreaking aspects of my own experience is that had the CPR worked, and the paramedics had managed to bring Shirley back, I know she would have hated them for it.

Chapter Thirteen
Sudoku weirdness

23rd August 09:26

I thought I ought to just acknowledge on here, the very weird thing that happened… a few days ago. In fact, Saturday the 19th August, to be exact. Beside the toilet here there is… there is the Radio Times. I keep it beside the toilet because I like to do the… the puzzles while sitting on the toilet. Some people read; I do puzzles. There you go. And when I got up on the morning of the 19th… I saw that… that various weird annotations had been made across one of the puzzle pages – specifically across the top centre box of the Sudoku. In my writing, across that box it says 'F'REVER'. F-apostrophe-R, E, V, E, R in capital letters… and then, immediately beneath that… in a very small cursive it says 'Barney', and there seems to be the number 7 next to it. It also appears that I've filled in some of those bits of Sudoku in a most bizarre way. I mean, numbers where they could not possibly be. I mean you know… I mean you know that you can't put, in this case, a 'one' on a line where there's another 'one'. And in this case, I've put a 'one' on a line where there is not only a 'one' going across, but a… a… a 'one' going down as well – so it's the most obvious place that I couldn't have put a 'one', and yet I seem to have put it there. As I said, this is all in my handwriting, yet I have absolutely no recollection of having written it, and why would I? Because it has destroyed the Sudoku, which I enjoy doing – and now I can't do that Sudoku because it's got this stuff all over it. It is bizarre… it wasn't there when I went to bed on Friday evening, but it's there when I got up on the Saturday morning. So there are… there's only one logical explanation, and that is that somehow I did it while sleepwalking. But I guess that would have meant I would have had to put the light on, taken the… taken the cap off the… off the pen, and… I mean, don't know, I can't explain it. As I say, the only logical explanation is that I did it while sleepwalking, but I have no recollection, and I have no idea why I would have done it. The other more fanciful… possibly, explanation is that it's some kind of message from beyond. The… clairvoyants and the… the spiritualists talk about automatic writing, when… the medium is not in control of their writing so although it's in their handwriting, it's from the other side, as it were. I find it interesting that the 'F'REVER' bit – F, apostrophe, R, E, V, E, R – is exactly how I used to write in Shirley's cards: 'Love you, f'rever and always', with the apostrophe instead of the o. But I don't know, I don't know… I'm completely at a loss to explain it. It is… just weird. It is just completely and utterly weird.

*

I'm not sure I can add anything to what I have explained in the recording. I have kept and laminated the page, because it is *so* bizarre, I thought that in years to come I might have grown to believe that I dreamed it. I have spoken to many people who have had strange experiences around the deaths of their loved ones – everything from just feeling their presence in a room to actually seeing them – but I've not had anything like that. Indeed, there are times when I've longed to feel her presence, but it has never happened. She has gone, and that is that. But this experience was the closest I've come (save for a couple of dreams, about which more later) to something that felt inexplicable.

When I spoke to my counsellor about this, however, he seemed to think that it was absolutely feasible that I had done it during an episode of sleepwalking, including putting on the light and uncapping the pen without waking myself, and while I was speaking to him about it, I remembered how I used to sleepwalk as a child, which I had all but forgotten about. So I guess I've got 'form' in this area, and that would be, as I've said, by far the most logical explanation.

The grieving mind can play some extraordinary tricks, of that I am sure. But to quote the Bard once again, "There are more things in Heaven and Earth, Horatio, than are dreamt of in your philosophy." [8]

And that is a sentiment with which I heartily concur.

Chapter Fourteen
From caterpillar to butterfly

28th August 07:41

Over the last weeks, my attention seems to have been drawn to moths and butterflies… some very beautiful ones, especially the Jersey Tiger moth, which I saw on a dog walk a few weeks ago. Then yesterday, I saw the most amazing little caterpillar just outside the church. It looked for all the world like a green leaf – and if it hadn't been moving that's what I would have thought it… it was. And this morning, as my thoughts roamed, I suddenly realised that there was a message in this. That a caterpillar has to pass through the pupation, the pupae, the pupa… or whatever it's called, in order to become the beautiful creature that it was aways intended to be. Even though the caterpillars themselves can be absolutely beautiful, that change that takes place – that rearrangement of the molecules and the atoms into something completely different – is a wonderful analogy of the passing from this world to the next. That we have to go through that death experience in order that we may become the beautiful creatures that we were always intended to be. And I guess there's a comfort in that.

*

This recording follows nicely on from the Shakespeare quote at the end of the last chapter, and begs the question: do I believe in an afterlife? In a realm or dimension beyond the here and now? The simple answer is that yes, I do, but Shirley's death has caused me to question much of what I thought I believed.

There was a time when I saw death in extraordinarily simplistic terms. I thought it would be like shedding your clothes and running naked into a sun-drenched meadow of fresh green grass, much like the obvious joy that cows feel when they are let out into the fields again after their winter confinement, leaping and frolicking like lambs in the lush spring grass. I spent some of my early, formative years on a farm, so this image is particularly vivid in my mind; an image of bucolic idealism worthy of the Romantics, but less than helpful in the middle of a cold, empty night when you are struggling to cope with the crippling waves of grief that pound away at your sanity.

I think the caterpillar analogy is a useful one though, for the caterpillar has no idea what lies in store for it as it responds to the physical/chemical stimuli that cause it to pupate – it simply submits to its fate as the natural order of things. Similarly, I don't believe we need to know or understand what happens after our death. We simply have to accept it as an experience that every one of us will have to go through, regardless of what may or may not lie beyond.

I discovered that I had jotted down the following in the 'notes' on my phone, though I forgot to put where it came from and a Google search failed to find it, so I apologise that I'm unable to credit it:

"We fear death not because this life is all there is, but because this is all we've known."

Setting aside any religious dogma for the moment, it has always seemed illogical to me that our brains are designed (or have evolved, if that's the way you prefer to think about it) to be such extraordinary repositories of experience, knowledge and wisdom, not to mention memories (treasured or otherwise), only for that wealth of information to be shut down and discarded at death. I know there will be many who are quite okay with that, and who would argue that once we are dead, we have no need of any of those things – so in the same way that our family will dispose of the physical possessions we have accumulated over our lifetime, so our memories are jettisoned at our death. The hard drive is wiped, as it were.

But that makes no sense to me. It seems an unfathomable waste of an existence. For me, a better analogy might be the way in which data is stored in 'the cloud' and survives somewhere out there on an unseen server even after the original devices that created that data are long gone. So yes, as I said earlier, I *do* believe in an afterlife, and I find it absolutely logical to do so – but what form that afterlife will take is anyone's guess.

Religion and philosophy have debated the question for millennia, and religious devotees – or followers of a specific school of philosophy– will firmly argue for the promises made by their own belief system. But when it comes to suicide, it seems to me that all religions flounder to reconcile modern, compassionate attitudes towards mental health with the more implacable teachings of their holy books. After all, it was not so very long ago that someone who had died by suicide couldn't be buried in consecrated ground, and it wasn't until 1983 that the Catholic church removed it from the list of mortal sins.

(It is also worth noting here that it was decriminalised in England and Wales in 1961 – 1966 in Northern Ireland – yet we still tend to speak of 'committing suicide' which is not only wrong but can be extremely hurtful to those who are dealing with the trauma of a loved one taking their own life. Be in no doubt that words matter.)

To nail my own colours to the mast, I have been a Christian since my late teens (mostly in that quiet, unassuming sort of way that the traditional Church of England has made its own), and we mustn't forget that Christianity was *founded* on the principle of life after death. That is what Easter is all about.

Which brings me full circle and makes it especially and cruelly ironic that Shirley took her life on Easter day.

Do I believe I will I see her again 'on the other side'? Shirley believed so, and my church would back up that belief absolutely, but in my current state of mind, I find myself conflicted. I used to think that the people who shared our earthly journey with us – family, friends, colleagues, acquaintances – were just that, fellow travellers along the road, but when we reached our final destination we would do so alone, and whatever lay beyond was so unlikely to bear any relation to what we have experienced here on earth, that the idea of being greeted by 'those who have gone before' was improbable at best.

Since Shirley died, however, I find myself desperate to believe that I will see her again, hoping with all my heart that we will find each other once more when my own time on earth is done – but unfortunately there can be no certainty on the subject.

In the gospel of Matthew, Jesus says that "in the resurrection, they neither marry nor are given in marriage, but are as the angels of God in heaven" [9] so read into that what you will.

Some weeks before she died, we were in the bedroom getting dressed when Shirley suddenly turned to me and said, "God hates me, doesn't He." The statement took me aback, and I shrugged it off with a simple "Of course He doesn't," but in truth, she deserved more of me than that. For at the heart of her question was an intensely personal outpouring of the ages-old conundrum: 'why does a supposedly loving God allow so much suffering?'

And I'm afraid it is a question to which I don't have an answer.

Chapter Fifteen
Roots & Wings

1st September 09:17

People ask me all the time, how am I doing? It's an interesting question. I know Shirley used to say that… that I would cope well, on my own. I'd be alright, was her phrase, and I guess that part of me also sort of thought I would. Many of the things I do weren't connected to Shirley… she didn't take part in them, and although our lives were inextricably linked, there were whole swathes of it that I just got on with. So yes, on the face of it, there is no reason why I wouldn't be able to survive without her. But… what I'm discovering now, of course, is that she enabled *all of those things… she empowered me to do them. She was the… well… to coin a phrase, she was the wind beneath my wings. She enabled me to fly. I used to do a talk which was about roots and wings. That in order to be able to fly, to really fly and achieve your potential you had to have your roots deep in something, whether that was your family, or… or a belief, or whatever, you had to have the roots in order to enable yourself to fly. And Shirley was my root, and my root has now been cut off. And so, I'm rather afraid that I am flightless.*

*

I feel I am letting her down, by not coping better. Though if you meet me in the street you wouldn't know that. The phrase I currently use to describe myself is 'outwardly managing, inwardly a mess,' but to be honest, I'm only *just* managing. Back in chapter six I described how adept I am at putting on a mask for those around me, and I have continued to do that as the months have passed. But the knowledge of just how badly I failed her and am still failing her; of what I could have done and *should* have done, piles up like Jenga around me, and I wonder how many more sticks it will take before it all comes crashing down.

One of the themes that run through these recordings is that of surprise that I am not coping better. Throughout my life I have always been so self-contained, so capable, so unfazed by whatever life might throw at me, that what I am experiencing now puts me in a place that is utterly alien to me. It is not who I am, and that has come as a profound shock that I don't seem to have the wherewithal to process.

I find it extraordinary that even now, a year later, I have been unable to bring myself to function as I did. I cast desperately about for anything that might enable me to recapture something of the joy and fulfilment I previously found in the things I used to do, but to no avail. Even throwing myself into new challenges has brought little interest and in truth just leaves me hollow, without much of a desire to continue.

Other than to fill the days.

And that, as I say, is an end in itself.

Chapter Sixteen
The Dream

3rd October 08:34

So it's been a little shy of six months now… just a few days shy of six months since Shirley passed away and for the first time I've been aware of dreaming of her. A simple little dream: we were at some Jubilee-style event, with military bands lining the streets, and we ducked through an… army outfitters, sort of a military outfitters, to get into the venue, which was a bit like a working men's club, actually. And we worked our way along the row until we were sitting more or less central so that we could see the stage, and then we became aware that we didn't have the cool box with us that had our food and drink in so I said I would go back to the car to get it, and I left her there in the row. There was more to the dream, but that was the bit that included Shirley. And I… when I woke, I was so grateful that I'd dreamt of her for the first time in all of these months. It just kind of felt lovely that we'd been somewhere together and shared something together, even though it was only in a dream.

*

At the end of this recording I had become very upset, and it ends abruptly. My voice had cracked, and I was physically and emotionally unable to record any more.

Such a short snippet of a dream, yet it is packed with so much poignancy. We used to do so much together, loved our trips out, whether locally or further afield, and I feel acutely the loss of that sharing and companionship. But here we were together again, just as it had been, and that meant more to me than you can ever know.

It also marked a very particular milestone. I had had such wonderful, vivid dreams in the months leading up to Shirley's death – so much so that I couldn't wait to get to sleep to experience them. In the months after she died, however, I had been unable to remember a single dream. It was like my sleep, as well as my waking hours, was empty.

Slowly, though, I began to remember snatches of dreams, but they never featured Shirley. It was as though even my unconscious was determined to show me that she had indeed gone, as though she had not only been erased from my life, but also from my dreams.

So this little dream, fleeting though it was, represented a way back. A mechanism by which, though not under my control, I could be with her again. And I don't have the words to express how wonderful that felt.

Chapter Seventeen
The Return

3rd October 08:36

I'm recording this a few days late, but having been to America, and had a bittersweet though mostly enjoyable time over there with my family… it was lovely to be in the bosom of my family, to be surrounded by people who accepted me and loved me… that was really lovely. But when I got back and I walked into the empty house, smelling musty because it had been shut up for a couple of weeks, I was… I'd never been so aware of how empty the house was, and how empty my life was – the house being a bit of a metaphor – and I realised that even though I put out this picture to the outside world that I'm coping, inside I am a complete and utter mess.

*

This was a bit of an unexpected visit. I have a large extended family in the States who I hadn't seen for almost two decades. Shirley and I had been intending to take the trip for several years, but the opportunity never presented itself, then Covid and lockdowns curtailed any such plans, and finally her illness put it off yet further.

After she had died my niece contacted me to send the family's condolences, and to tell me I would be welcome any time, which was lovely of them, but I didn't feel ready for such a solo adventure at that stage. She persisted (not in a pressured way, just letting me know that their door was always open), finally suggesting that it might be combined with her mother's (my sister's) birthday, which falls at the beginning of August. I had already accepted a bit of work over the summer which meant that was out of the question, but we settled on my going over in mid-September, and with an impressive bit of jiggery-pokery, she managed to postpone my sister's birthday celebrations by five weeks. She also managed to keep my visit a total secret from the rest of the family (quite how I'll never know) so that when I made my entrance to the party it came as complete surprise to everyone.

It was, of course, a bittersweet journey, as Shirley should have been there with me, and I'd be lying if I said I didn't shed a great many tears while I was there, but it was lovely to see them all and to be so well received by everyone. They all looked after me wonderfully and I am so very grateful to them all for making the trip so memorable.

A good friend told me that as Shirley lived forever in my heart, I would be taking her with me wherever I went, and that's a comforting thought, even if I don't always feel it. At the risk of repeating myself, I knew she was gone from the very first and have never had that experience of feeling her presence that others say they have had about their lost loved ones. I do talk to her every day, though – even though I know she's not there – and that simple action helps me feel far less alone.

But as I say in this recording, I really wasn't prepared for the shock of returning to a musty, empty house, where not even Barney was there to greet me. In fact, I basically just dropped my bags, opened a few windows, then rushed around to my dog-sitters to collect my little boy and bring him home. I couldn't bear to be alone in the house longer than I absolutely had to be.

(I do have to say that I am blessed with the nicest people as dog-sitters. All the while I was in America they kept me up to date with how he was doing, and sent me various photos of him thoroughly enjoying life. They understood how anxious I was about leaving him, and I am extremely thankful for the way they made that so easy for me.)

The other thing that occurred soon after my return from America was the inquest into Shirley's death. I had been informed just before I left (I actually got the call while I was on the train to Heathrow) that the coroner had decided that her case was a very straightforward one – in that there was no doubt as to the cause of death – so could be dealt with by a 'documentary' inquest, that is to say no witnesses needed to be called and the documents pertaining to the case would simply be read out in open court. Because of this, they were able to bring the date forward. I was told I could attend if I wished, but there was no requirement for me to do so, and to my eternal regret I decided not to put myself through the ordeal. In retrospect, I wish I had been braver and gone along, regardless of how emotionally difficult it promised to be. It was an important stage in the story of Shirley's death, and I should have been there. Just one more thing to beat myself up about.

    I managed to put it to the back of my mind while I was away, but lying on the mat as I opened the door of my musty, empty house was an A4 envelope containing all the witness statements, the results of the post-mortem, and sundry other documents. It took me several days before I plucked up the courage to go through them. Professional and to the point, the words swam before my eyes like scripts from a TV courtroom drama – as though they were something far removed from me, something that belonged to an alternate reality, a surrealist nightmare worthy of Dali or Bunuel. As I waded through the pages, I discovered details of her death that I simply had not known, a slew of new information that I was suddenly forced to come to terms with.

Believe me when I tell you that I simply cannot find the words to describe how emotionally harrowing it was to read through the contents of that envelope. Thinking of it now, all the horror of that moment has come crashing back, and I am sobbing once again, sobbing uncontrollably. It was the hardest thing I have ever had to read.

A couple of weeks later I received a bland letter from the coroner giving me the verdict of the inquest and expressing sympathy for my loss. The letter summed up her death in just three words: 'due to suicide.'

And that was that.

Chapter Eighteen
Six months

11th October 20:30

So we are now a couple of days after the six month anniversary of Shirley's passing. I have a terrible cold, so I apologise for my voice, but since I'm probably going to be the only one who hears it, it hardly matters. There's only two things I wanted to say… one is that throughout the last weekend Barney hurt himself somehow, I don't know quite how, but because he was feeling in pain and poorly, he took himself off to the bedroom, and sat underneath where Shirley's jacket is hanging on the wardrobe. He just wanted to be close to his mum, because he was hurting, and that broke my heart.

The other thing I wanted to say was that I'm finding it hard to remember Shirley when I try to remember places we've been and things that we've done. I find it difficult to bring her to mind. I can remember the photos that we took, I can remember her in the photos. When I think of something like, you know, our trip to Rome, I can see her in the photos that we took in Rome. What I can't do is bring her to mind outside of those photos, and that is bizarre and somewhat upsetting.

*

The first part of this recording follows on from the sentiments I expressed in the last chapter (and elsewhere in this book) concerning my anxiety around Barney and his health. Dachshunds are well-known for developing back problems, and all the time we have had him it has been a constant worry, especially since he is a bit of a daredevil and leaps up onto and down from horribly high steps, walls, and pieces of furniture. He was therefore living on borrowed time and sure enough, he must have landed awkwardly and strained his back.

Luckily, he was back to his normal self within a couple of days without having to resort to the vet, but it was a worrying forty-eight hours.

The second part refers to a strange phenomenon that, thankfully, seems to be improving. The thought that I might never be able to bring those memories to mind, painful though they may be, upset me so much that I couldn't bear to imagine a life where that might continue. I have surrounded myself with photos of her, and I find that comforting, but it was the memories that I was missing, as though my mind had deliberately blanked them out, which I now think was almost certainly the case.

I remember very early on in this process, a wonderful friend of mine who could not have been more supportive – even though he subsequently had his own serious health problems to deal with – suggested that perhaps it was unhelpful to have so many photos around, and that it might be better to put some of them away for a while. I politely pointed out that that wasn't ever going to happen.

I understand exactly why he thought that it might help, but it comes back to the central tenet of grief, that everyone deals with it in their own way, and we all must find our own path through. There is no right or wrong way to go about it, but I can assure you that it soon becomes apparent what best works for you… and equally, what doesn't.

Chapter Nineteen
Facing The Future… the day after

1st November 08:29

I am continually amazed by the different ways that grief takes you. Yesterday was not a good day. It wasn't a horrible sort of keening pain that I've had so often during this horrible, horrible period… it was just a deep-seated, low-level sadness which had just gripped me all day. Now I don't know whether it was… it was triggered by the fact that the night before I had had the first of my 'Face The Future' sessions with Samaritans, but it may also have been because now we've put the clocks back everything is very dark and dismal, and it was a very, very overcast, rainy, horrible day. But, yeah, I just felt very down… very sad… very alone… and bereft.

*

Throughout this process I have been supported by Dorset Open Door[10] who I cannot recommend highly enough. They were initially suggested to me by my doctor in the first week after Shirley died, and for the next six months they rang me every week without fail, to find out how I was, to give me the chance to talk, and to vent if I needed it. After that they fixed me up with a peer support mentor, who has been wonderful, as well as keeping up telephone contact as and when it was required. They have quite literally been a lifesaver.

It was Open Door who suggested that I apply for the 'Facing the Future'[11] course, run by the Samaritans,[12] and which is specifically for people who have been bereaved by suicide. I was, as you might expect, a little nervous about the first session, but the others on the course were so lovely, and the facilitators so good, that my fears soon evaporated. With no set syllabus to follow, we were encouraged simply to talk to each other, to share our experience, and to be mutually supportive. Even so, just having to be so open and honest about what had happened was extremely challenging and resulted in quite a negative reaction the following day, as the recording reveals.

I have to say, though, that as the course progressed (it ran for six consecutive weeks) and we all got to know each other, it became, in a strange way, something to look forward to. Just knowing that you were with a group of people who knew exactly where you were coming from was a wonderful relief, and, though we don't post all that often these days, some of us have continued to keep in touch via a WhatsApp group.

I would recommend the course wholeheartedly.

Chapter Twenty
The voice in the morning

2nd November 16:38

So when I awoke this morning, I heard a woman's voice calling my name. I, of course, thought it was Shirley. It was probably some remnant of a dream as I woke up. I've heard people say that sometimes when you wake up you expect the other person to be there and then when they're not it's like another bereavement all over again. I can see what they mean. Later on this morning I was driving through town and I saw the back of somebody wearing the identical rain jacket that Shirley used to wear, her red one, and that made me start to well up and all I could think was: 'This is just going to keep happening isn't it, over and over again, and I'm never gonna be free of it.'

*

People have continually told me that it will get easier, and looking back over the last year, I can see that in many respects it has. I am no longer in floods of tears every day, though it still hits me when I am least expecting it. I can concentrate on things far better now, as this little book testifies. I find it easier to be in company, and can even laugh at people's jokes, though I still make sure I have an 'escape plan' so I can duck out when it starts to be too much. So all-in-all, I can see that there has been definite progress.

As a corollary to this, I have been aware that I am continually writing about the fact that I no longer find joy in anything, but I think for the purposes of this book I need to make a distinction between joy and pleasure. I would define 'joy' as a feeling that bubbles up from the heart, and which infuses your mind and body with an extraordinary sense of wellbeing – so much so that it can spill over, affecting those around you, and invoking an almost childlike state of enjoyment, wonder, and laughter. It invariably results in broad smiles and twinkling eyes.

Pleasure, on the other hand, comes from simple enjoyment of the things you do or the things you experience. Enjoying a delicious meal, for example, or watching your children at play. It would be wrong to suggest that I can no longer take pleasure in such things – though it is probably more muted than before – but I long for the day when I can once again experience real joy.

Similarly, I still can't work up much enthusiasm for anything, still get strange jittery attacks of nerves (I hesitate to call them panic attacks, though I suspect they are related), still feel lost and alone, and still can't see a positive future, so there remains a long way to go.

It also remains the case that I haven't been able to bring myself to get rid of any of Shirley's things. There are of course many reasons for this, and some I have already spoken about. But looking at the last couple of sentences in this recording, I am reminded that one of the reasons for not taking bags of her clothes down to the local charity shops is that to do so would run the risk of seeing people out and about in town wearing her clothes, and I don't think I could cope with that.

Chapter Twenty-One
Not just grief

2nd November 22:00

It's not just the grief – or rather it is – but all of my emotions are so close to the surface that anything... apart from joy of course, I can't take joy in anything at the moment... but all the other emotions are so easily triggered. Things that normally I could take in my stride I just can't anymore – they just overwhelm me. I get annoyed, frustrated... upset, obviously, at the tiniest little things.

*

As I have said before, one of the unforeseen consequences of this new emotional reality is reflected in the amount of work that I can take on. On the one hand, I find that work is a wonderful distraction and occupies my hours so that I can't dwell on the grief; but on the other, I need to give myself plenty of time for the preparation for each job, so that I do not become overwrought or unduly stressed. This is a huge change from how I used to be, when I could gather my things and go off to a gig pretty much at a moment's notice and would think nothing of taking a couple of bookings on the same day. Now I have to be absolutely sure of every aspect of the job, have to feel totally prepared and in control, or my stress levels will start to rocket. The upshot of this is that I have effectively gone from three or four jobs a week to three or four jobs a month, which has, of course, had a major impact on my earning potential, but at the moment it is the only way I can function. We all have to find our own way to make life manageable as we pick our way through, and this works for me.

There is a poem, published on Facebook by Elena Mikhalkova, called 'The Room of Ancient Keys'[13] which seems pertinent to this, and which runs as follows:

> My grandmother once gave me a tip:
> In difficult times, you move forward in small steps.
> Do what you have to do, but little by little.
> Don't think about the future, or what may happen tomorrow.
> Wash the dishes.
> Remove the dust.
> Write a letter.
> Make a soup.
> You see?
> You are advancing step by step.
> Take a step and stop.
> Rest a little.
> Praise yourself.
> Take another step.
> Then another.
> You won't notice, but your steps will grow more and more.
> And the time will come when you can think about the future without crying.

Chapter Twenty-Two
Sobbing

5th November 16:25

This morning I wept uncontrollably in a way that I haven't done for months now. Normally what I've... what happens is that something triggers it and I well up, tears come but within a very short period of time I'm able to control it and fight it back. This morning I just sobbed and sobbed and sobbed. What was the trigger for it? I was just playing with Barney. There's a.... almost everything about Barney triggers it because he is absolutely essential to my relationship with Shirley. We chose him together, she used to say that he was the child we never had, and I sort of... you know, can see that and go along with that. And now, of course, there's just me and him, and... yeah... so this morning it just overwhelmed me and I just... huge, deep, wracking sobs for quite a while before I could bring myself out of it.

*

"If the people are buying tears, I'll be rich someday, ma."[14]

As soon as I had listened again to this entry, the above lyric jumped into my head. It is from the American folk singer Melanie who sadly passed away at the beginning of 2024. I have always had a love of her powerful, quirky, intoxicating songs, and when Shirley died I gravitated towards her double album 'Four Sides of Melanie' which is a compilation album (essentially a 'Best of...') and features a wonderful collection of her music, much of which I found perfectly suited to my mood. Over the last year I have continued to return to it, and have wept along with her beautiful lyrics day after day after day.

But what I say in this recording raises a more fundamental issue: how something you can love so completely (in this case, Barney) can also be a cause of so much pain, through no fault of its own, but purely because it throws up so many memories of the time – and the person –that has gone. Like the photographs that bring cascades of tears whenever I look at them, so dear, sweet little Barney is also a cause of so much heartache. Yet these things are so precious to me I couldn't dream of parting with them, not *in spite* of the pain they cause, but *because* of it. That something can be at the same time both a source of heart-wrenching pain *and* the most extraordinary comfort is something I could not have believed had I not experienced it myself. And it falls to me to find a way to manage that pain, so that I can keep these precious memories central to my life.

We had been looking for a dachshund for several years when Shirley found Barney on Facebook. They so rarely come up on rescue or rehoming sites that we had all but given up, determined as we were that we wanted a rescue dog. We arranged to go over to see him and were greeted by a barking ball of fluff that captured our hearts instantly – and more importantly, he seemed to take immediately to us, too. His owner, thankfully, also liked us, and she instructed us to go away and think about whether we wanted him, assuring us that she would not give him to anyone else until she had heard back from us. We drove a short way down the road to a pub where we ordered lunch, sat down, then shared a look that said what we were both thinking. Just to be sure I voiced that thought. "We're going to have him, aren't we?"

"Of course we are… phone her now!" came the reply, and before our food had arrived we had agreed to pick him up the following weekend.

He jumped into our car without so much as a look back and the rest, as they say, is history. Once we arrived home, he ran to our front door as though he had lived there all his life, and he has proved a better companion than we could ever have dreamed. For us he was, and remains to this day, the perfect dog.

And through these darkest of times, he has been my saviour.

Chapter Twenty-Three
A bad start

8th November 09:33

This morning is not a good morning. I woke up feeling just so grief-stricken. I couldn't face the day really, is the truth. I was in tears and it's not… it's not that I can't come to terms with the fact that Shirley is no longer with me: I know that. I mean logically and absolutely I know that, and I know that there is no way that anything can change that fact, and so… so I have to try and find a way forward. I suppose that the worst thing about that is that I still can't see a way of making life better. I can only see that it is going to continue like this. I can't even describe myself as lonely, really, because it's so much more than that. It's not just… it's not lonely… it's… it's just this profound, profound sense of loss that I can't pull myself out of. I don't know, I just… I've said before that there is no joy in my life, in anything I do. I'm just simply using up the minutes, and the seconds, and the hours, from getting up to going to bed. I'm quite good at filling that and other people seem to be coming together to fill those… that time for me too, so it's not that I'm not busy… it's just that there is no motivation or enthusiasm for any of it. And I don't know how I'm ever going to shake this off. I don't know how I'm ever going to manage to go forward, to go forward with any sense of purpose or… or joy.

*

Throughout this recording runs a quiet desperation. Will it ever get any better? Or is this my life now? Once I had reached the milestone of the first year anniversary (the point at which I stopped recording these thoughts and feelings) I fell into an eerily calm acceptance of what I had been through. It felt as though I had turned a corner in my journey through grief and could start to think more positively about the future.

The feeling lasted about two days, before the most crushing wave of grief broke over me, and my mood plummeted. I had no idea where this had come from, there being no obvious triggers, but on teasing it out with my counsellor, we decided that possibly it was the realisation that having survived the first year, I now had to embark upon my second. Reaching the first anniversary had been an unconscious goal, and the very fact that life was, in some senses, returning to a kind of 'normal' itself posed a huge psychological challenge. I was going through the motions of life as it used to be, but without Shirley there to give it any meaning.

Jamie Anderson, writer, poet, and speaker is the author of one of those quotes that are continually appearing on the internet, yet few people know from whom they originate. The full quote runs as follows:

> "Grief, I've learned, is really just love.
> It's all the love you want to give, but cannot. All that unspent love gathers up in the corners of your eyes, the lump in your throat, and in that hollow part of your chest. Grief is just love with no place to go." [15]

It is that last line which is best known… and which utterly breaks my heart.

Chapter Twenty-Four
Robins

8th November 09:38

I'm not sure that I've recorded this before, so I'm going to do it now, and if it turns out that I have then I'll delete one of them, but I want to talk about my robin experiences. There is a folklore, old wives' tale if you like, that if a robin appears, a loved one is near... and I've had two robin experiences. The first one was quite early on, when I took… when I was taking Barney for walks at a distance from home so that I wouldn't bump into anybody, because I couldn't face anybody in those first few weeks, and so I took him over to Corfe Castle and we were walking down by the river and we passed a place where, very early on in our relationship – the second time, that is – Shirley and I went for a picnic right by the river and it was the most glorious day, and the sun was dappling through the leaves, and it was just magical. Anyway, we… Barney and I walked past that place, and now they've made it into a proper picnic place – it wasn't then, we just sat by the river   but now there are actual picnic tables, and we sat down at one of these picnic tables and I had a little weep, and suddenly a robin came hopping along, not at all bothered by the fact I had Barney with me and Barney wasn't bothered by the robin. And the robin hopped up onto the table and just stayed there and chirruped at me, just… just… just chatted at me for, oh, a good five minutes, until finally we said goodbye to the robin and went on our way. Whether that was coincidence or anything to do with Shirley who will ever know, but I found it quite comforting at the time.

And the second one was not so very long ago. I was walking Barney down the… down the… the little alleyway thing that goes… goes to the north of the park. And we walk there every day really, even if we're going somewhere longer we'll… we'll walk… we'll walk down that little path. And a little robin came, and again came ridiculously close to me – I mean, right up to my face really. I even put my finger out to see if it would jump onto my finger 'cos it was that close and seemingly tame, but it didn't, it just looked at my finger and stayed there. But again, it just chatted and chatted and chatted at me for… for several minutes before… before Barney became fractious at the fact we hadn't moved in a while and his movement then spooked the robin and off it flew. But again, very interesting to… to think that perhaps there's something in those old wives' tales after all.

*

Over the years I have had quite a lot to do with the English Folk tradition and have always loved these little snippets of folklore that seem to have doggedly survived the onslaught of science and technology. In a world where phenomena can be increasingly explained by the furious pace of advances in human understanding, there is something comforting in these echoes of a simpler, more poetic outlook on life.

A little while ago I spoke to a woman who said she liked to believe that whenever she saw a random white feather it indicated that her late husband was sending her comfort. From the moment of his death, she had meticulously saved every feather she saw in two large glass jars.

Another told me that she collected shells to remind her of happy days spent walking the seashore with her lost loved ones. These were her 'happy shells' and would be kept, but those she collected on days when she felt particularly affected by the weight of her grief would be her 'unhappy shells', which she would throw back into the sea in the hope that they might later become 'happy shells' for someone else.

There are so many ways that we seek to find comfort in the everyday, and as always, there is no right or wrong strategy to cope with your grief. It's whatever works for you. Whether you look to old beliefs and folklore; take what joy you can in the natural world around you; listen on a loop to a piece a music you once shared together; cry on the shoulder of a trusted friend; or simply rage against the cruelty of God, we all need to find our own way to manage this dreadful new reality that we have been plunged into.

For at the end of the day, we can do nothing to change it.

And that's the awful truth.

Chapter Twenty-Five
A milestone of sorts

12th November 14:03

And suddenly here we are in week thirty. I'm aware that saying that it makes it sound like I'm describing the stages of a pregnancy, although in this case, of course, there is no happy event to look forward to at week forty. However, there have been a couple of little milestones. The first was that last Friday was the first day in this entire thirty weeks when I didn't cry. I've been sort of waiting for that day, the day when I didn't cry. I've been telling everyone all the way through there hasn't been a day when I... when I haven't cried at some point or another, and last Friday was it. Of course, then Saturday I was triggered by a piece of music and I was in hopeless sobs again, so there's still a long, long way to go. But a sort of milestone.

The other sort of milestone was that I haven't... been dreaming of Shirley. I think I had one short dream in which she figured, and it made me feel very happy to be with her, even if only in a dream and for a very short time. I think I've already recorded a piece about that. But I've had two more very, very short dreams – not dreams about her, but dreams in which she is... for a short time, but nevertheless she is there... and I do find those strangely comforting. And I hope... I hope that's gonna continue and develop because as I think I've said before, sleep is, for me, really the only escape. I'm so lucky that I have managed to continue sleeping pretty well all the way through this awful process, so to encounter Shirley in my dream, even for a very, very tiny amount of time, is a lovely thing.

*

Though we had thirteen wonderful years together, I have been shocked at how quickly that precious time is fading into the past. It is almost like our time together was indeed a dream, rather than the glorious reality that it was.

> "We are such things as dreams are made on, and our little life is rounded in a sleep."[16]

The more I struggle to hold on to the detail of those years, the more I become appalled at how much time we wasted on the minutiae of life – on dealing with things which suddenly seem to have been of no value. There is so much inconsequential rubbish in our lives to which we seem to be oblivious while we are in the thick of it, but when we look back we can see for what it is – the most colossal waste of the fleeting time we have been granted.

In 'Big Yellow Taxi' Joni Mitchell famously utters the line "Don't it always seem to go… that you don't know what you've got till it's gone…"[17] Well, I absolutely knew what I had – having let it slip through my fingers once already – but there were still so many times when I let other 'stuff' get in the way.

Nowadays, when friends have anniversaries my overriding wish for them is that they should cherish each other, because the time they have is so incredibly precious, and can be whisked away in a second.

And if you're reading this and are fortunate enough to still have the love of your life by your side, then that is what I wish for you, too. With all of my heart.

Chapter Twenty- Six
Dreams

20th November 11:45

As I've recorded before, for the first few months after Shirley died, I couldn't remember any dreams at all, it seemed like I wasn't dreaming at all. And then I started dreaming again, getting a few… remembering a few vivid dreams, but Shirley was very rarely, if ever, in them, and when she was in them it was always just a short, fleeting thing. Last night I had a dream which was kind of extraordinary. I was with a woman – I don't know who she was, she's not one of my friends, she's no one that I actually know – she had a young boy of probably about sort of eight… seven or eight, and I was playing with him as though he were my son, and when I reached out to hold her hand I got a terrific… a terrific warm buzz of love just washed… washed through me, and I actually said to her in the dream, "What's happening?" 'cos I couldn't believe that I was having this feeling of love emanating. Now I don't know what… you know… I don't know what that is supposed to mean. I don't know… I don't know, I originally… immediately I thought, I felt guilty because I was with someone else and feeling love for someone else. What the dream is trying to tell me I just don't know, but I record it here because it is one of those little moments that has… that has imprinted itself upon my brain.

*

I still have no idea who the woman in the dream might have been, but it occurs to me that when my ex-wife (the woman I was married to before Shirley and I got back together) and I started seeing each other, she had a seven-year-old son, so perhaps my subconscious was dredging that up, at least in part.

The obvious implication of the dream is to tell me that I *could* find love again, possibly, but I'm certainly nowhere near that place as yet and find it hard to imagine that I ever could be. But I guess we should never say never.

While she was ill, Shirley used to say to me that if anything happened to her, I should find someone else – in fact, she would often say that I could find someone better. My reply was always the same: that I'd been there, tried that, and had proved to myself that there *couldn't* be anyone better. She was the only one for me, my soulmate and the love of my life, and I should have realised that before I let her go in the first place.

People often talk about their 'other half.' I believe it goes back to the story of Adam and Eve (Eve being created from Adam's rib), the implication being that we are somehow split from our soulmate at birth, and we strive to find them again throughout our lives.

It's hard to see that there's any truth to this idea, but I can understand where it comes from – because if we are lucky, we will find someone who so completes us that it is like we were always destined to be together.

I can honestly say that Shirley and I were two such people.

And that just makes the loss of her all the more acute.

Chapter Twenty-Seven
Life expands

28th November 19:17

They say that life expands around the grief – the grief doesn't get any smaller, but life expands around it – and I guess this week has sort of been an example of that. My work has picked up, I'm still not doing as much as I used to, but… but enough, so that I'm not stressed and I've got plenty of time to prepare for each job. So it's been a busy week. I've also had little Barney to contend with because he hurt his back, so I've been backwards and forwards to the vet and he's full of painkillers and because he's no longer in pain he thinks he's perfectly alright and can do everything, so he's been a real worry this week. So with the work and the worry things have been very busy and life has indeed expanded. Then today I got my first Christmas card of the season, and it was from the funeral directors, inviting me, amongst other things, to… if I wished to… put a message or a bauble or something on their tree of remembrance. It hit me quite hard getting that card and I mean, I know they did it from the best possible motives… they say in the card how difficult the first Christmas is, but it was a real blow to the stomach to get it and to open it, and I just crumbled. So, yes, life may be expanding around the grief, but the grief absolutely doesn't get any less. The grief sits there like a great black brooding presence… and you can turn away from it a bit, and you can ignore it a little bit – as the months go by that becomes slightly easier to do – but it's always there and then it just rises up and bites you.

*

Julia Samuel[18] says that grief is a neat and tidy word for something that is chaotic and messy, and she's right. I've been told that when a loved one dies, the grief can be like a bomb going off and peppering your body with thousands of shards of glass, which you then spend year after year after year slowly trying to pick out – and no matter how well you think you're doing, how many shards you've managed to remove, there's always another one lodged deep inside, which makes its presence felt when you least expect it.

Sometimes there's an obvious trigger, like the sudden arrival of the Christmas card, but more often than not it will just hit you out of the blue, and that's the hardest one to cope with.

Thinking about it now, I guess that the problem with Barney's back could also be seen as a metaphor – while he was dosed up on painkillers he thought the pain had gone, only to have it return with a vengeance just when he had started to believe he was fine.

That's the trouble with grief, everything's a bloody metaphor. Good ways to think about it, perhaps, but none of them actually help to take the pain away.

Of the many 'Grief Poets' that seem to flood social media with their work (or flood mine, at any rate, algorithms being what they are), sara rian[19] (she doesn't capitalise her name... a small affectation no doubt, along the lines of e.e.cummings) is one whose imagery often chimes with me. In her poem *grief is love*, she has the following lines:

"grief is a bleeding hand
holding a stem full of thorns

being told to focus on the rose."

With this poem fresh in my mind, I found myself reading an article in which the writer discussed the problems that often arise from society's obsession with being positive about everything. It struck a chord with me because not so long ago my therapist took me through the concept of 'sitting with your grief,' an exercise which initially I found so painful I thought it would destroy me.

The idea is that instead of trying to find distractions from your grief, you should allow it to wash over and through you, like the onrush of a tidal wave. She described grief as a diva, a prima donna who demands to be centre stage, demands your full attention, and the more you deny it that role, the more it will come at you. So her advice was to give it what it craves, allow it to strut its stuff in front of you, for only then will it begin to wear itself out, like a toddler having a tantrum.

I was told to try the exercise for a short time at first, and I was happy to follow her advice, but when the next wave hit, it so overwhelmed me that I had no choice but to let it run its course. Stopping after a set time had elapsed was simply not an option. And once it had passed, the aftereffects lingered through the rest of the day.

sara rian is right. It's impossible to focus on the rose when you are in such horrific pain, no matter how much people may encourage you to.

There are times when it's simply not possible to be positive, and that's okay.

Perhaps as a society we need to learn take that on board.

Chapter-Twenty-Eight
Triggers, triggers, triggers

29th November 10:40

So this morning's trigger was putting on my wedding ring – or rather not my wedding ring, because I never take that off – but Shirley's wedding ring. Ever since she passed away, I've been wearing her wedding ring on a leather strap around my neck. Take it off at night, put it on again in the morning. This morning, for some reason, when I picked it up to put it on, I just was transported straight back to our wedding day, and I was just in floods of tears remembering how lovely that was…

*

Following on from the last chapter, here I am talking about triggers, and none more guaranteed to hit like a juggernaut than memories of our wedding day.

It was the most beautiful, simple day – exactly how we wanted it to be – no fuss, but an endless quantity of love and joy. We had arranged to do it while on holiday in Swanage, with a blessing in our local church when we got back to which family and friends were invited, and it couldn't have been more perfect. The sun shone, and we walked down to Swanage town hall where we went through the formalities before entering the chamber to become husband and wife. Just six of us, plus the registrar and her assistant, a soundtrack that we had carefully chosen from our favourite music, simple vows, and smiles that lit up the room.

Afterwards we went across to the Purbeck Hotel for lunch, then a quick change followed by a walk on the beach and a paddle in the sea. As I said, perfect.

When she decided that she could go on no longer, and went out to end her life, Shirley left all of her possessions – phone, purse, jewellery – behind in the bedroom, as I later discovered. Once the police had gone, I found a length of leather shoelace and fastened her wedding ring about my neck, vowing to her that it would always be against my heart.

And so it has been.

And so it always will be.

I believe psychologists talk of such things as 'touchstones' – a physical talisman to keep the person close, and which can be touched at times of great grief or stress to bring some form of comfort and relief to the wearer. That makes sense, I suppose, and is a neat explanation of a common human behavioural trait, from a baby's comfort blanket to wearing a St Christopher or fiddling with prayer beads. But all I know is that from that very first moment, I felt the need to wear her ring, that profound symbol of our love for and commitment to one another, a love and commitment that even the finality of death cannot take away.

The traditional Christian wedding service talks about 'till death us do part' as though that's the end of our commitment, but love does not turn off like a lightbulb when a partner dies – rather it burns more brightly, fuelled by everything you want to say to them; everything you want to share with them; everything you want to apologise for. In short, everything you want to do and say which you will never have the chance to do and say ever again.

Jamie Anderson[15] is quite right when she says, "Grief is just love with no place to go."

Instead, it bubbles up from deepest depths of your soul, rips through your heart and mind, spills from your eyes and nose and mouth… and in the rawness of a pain for which there are simply no words, just howls, and howls, and howls.

Chapter Twenty-Nine
Stealth attack

7th December 17:34

Tonight, I'm feeling particularly down. I don't know why… it's not been a bad day. I've been out to lunch with a group of colleagues, and we've had a really nice time with really nice food. I've come home, I had to take Barney to the vets – I mean I was hoping he'd have a clean bill of health and I'd be able to walk him again, but she says she doesn't want him to have any of that kind of exercise for at least a fortnight so that has sort of knocked me back a bit. But I don't know… I don't know where this sudden attack of grief has come from. It's very debilitating… I feel very low indeed… I don't know, I just don't know. I've made myself a bit of tea even though I didn't want it because I had such a lovely lunch, but I thought, well, that's something I can do to take my mind off things… and I've now resorted to gin. It is such an awful thing, this. Such an awful thing.

*

I mentioned previously (in chapter twenty-six) that Barney had hurt his back. It is a constant worry with Dachshunds, with their long backs and little legs, so it was an anxious time. After a couple of days during which he didn't want to move, let alone jump anywhere, I had taken him to the vets who thought that he hadn't done anything terrible, just sprained the muscles, but ordered complete crate rest for four weeks and pumped him full of painkillers. She also said that the previous bout of back pain he'd had would have been a warning, and that I needed to be much more vigilant about his movements in future. And that meant NO JUMPING!

Even though I knew the vet had his best interests at heart, I didn't have it in me to restrict him to his crate for such a long time, so I allowed him to move about the house, but put bags and boxes on the furniture so that he wasn't tempted to try to jump up, and bought a ramp so that he could still access his favourite chair. The ramp was a great success, so I soon invested in another, making my small front room look like a screenshot from Tetris.

Unfortunately, the lack of dog walking for a month not only meant that Barney put on a bit of weight, but I did too, and as we were fast approaching Christmas, that was not a good thing.

I also note the reference to gin here. When Shirley was alive, we drank very little – a gin and tonic on a Friday tea-time, sometimes a shared bottle of wine over the course of a weekend, and the occasional sherry. As a student I had drunk a lot of beer (as you might expect...), but once I'd started working I was driving most of the time, so just got out of the habit. But since Shirley died, I have been drinking a little more. Not huge amounts, but I have a beer with my dinner most nights, and I still like to have a gin on a Friday – in homage to my former life – though I always perform a toast to Shirley when I do, and it always has me in tears.

Chapter Thirty
Nearly 9 months on and still a mess

12th December 09:24

It's nine months… nine months on and I'm still a mess. This morning I was having my usual morning snuggle with my little dog Barney, and I was just trying to joke with him about the fact that it was my birthday next week, just exactly a week's time, and I was saying to him how "I hope you've got me something nice"… and then the realisation of it… that this will be the first birthday without Shirley. And I know that traditionally I've always worked on my birthday except for a couple of… a couple of times, so never made a really big deal about it, but for some reason this morning it just absolutely hit me, and it all came tumbling down again. It's very easy to think that this is never ever going to end.

*

The first thing to point out here is that this recording was *not* made at the nine-month point, but rather at eight months. Another example of my grief-addled brain clouding my sense of time.

I also note that the grief hit me after I had been talking to Barney about my birthday. As I say in the recording, I have never been in the habit of marking my birthday – even when I was growing up, because my birthday is so close to Christmas, no one made a fuss of it – and when I started working, the run-up to Christmas was always a particularly busy time, so again, the day passed without ceremony. But Shirley used to like to spoil me a little, even to the extent where one year we took a trip to Amsterdam for the Christmas market, which was a beautiful, joyous experience, and one of the best birthdays I have ever had.

Of course, this particular birthday marked the beginning of a run of special occasions, none of which I was looking forward to. Christmas, New Year, the anniversary of our moving to Dorset, Shirley's birthday and Valentine's Day were all coming up like a succession of speeding trains, and I was standing on the tracks, unable to get out of their way.

They say that such occasions are always the hardest, and with so many bearing down on me, I had no idea how I was going to cope.

It should also be noted that I say I had been *talking* to Barney. Since the very first day after Shirley's death, I have been continually talking while I'm in the house – to Shirley, to Barney, to myself, to God – and although it doesn't stop the tears from falling (in fact, as in the example above, it is often the *cause* of the tears), I find it extremely comforting, as it makes me feel far less alone.

And anything that does that has got to be a good thing.

Chapter Thirty-One
Bittersweet distractions

28th December 09:05

So it's the twenty-eighth of December, coming up to thirty-eight weeks since Shirley left us. Christmas is over... it's been a lovely distraction. Bittersweet, but nonetheless, as good a time as I could have hoped to have had. Amongst other... what most people would think of as joys... is the fact that my son and his partner are going to be getting married. He proposed yesterday, and so that's lovely. And they're also expecting their first child, which will be my first grandchild, so again it's a bittersweet distraction. Whenever I do things and hear things like this I always think of how much Shirley would have loved it, and how much I would have loved for Shirley to be part of it, but of course she isn't, and so it is just a distraction. It would be joyful, if I could summon up any joy, but joy is completely missing from my life as I have said before. There is no joy any more... there is just... there is just getting through the days, putting one foot in front of the other – this is all stuff that I've said so many times before. So this is the state I'm in. Yesterday I pinched a photo that I'd seen on Facebook and posted it on my feed... it was just a piece of electrical equipment with a label on it saying: 'I'm still working, but my light has gone out'. And that absolutely sums it up. There is no better way of saying it. 'I am still working, but my light has gone out'. And I cannot see... I have no idea when and if that light might start to flicker again. And in the meantime, we're coming into a new year. I can't say I'm sad to see the old one go.

*

I have always loved Christmas, yet over the years I have had many that were less than joyous occasions, sometimes because of things that had happened which eclipsed the joy of the season, or more often than not because I was in a difficult relationship at the time.

I remember when I was a youngster, I would work out how many Christmases I would have if I lived to a certain age, and as each year passed, I would think 'only x number left to go.' So it was always painful to me when my Christmases didn't live up to their promise. But I never let that dampen my enthusiasm for them.

When Shirley and I got back together, Christmases took on a new meaning – we had missed out on so many that I wanted each one from that point on to be a wonderful experience, and the fact that Shirley seemed to be scarred from her own past Christmas experiences made me all the more determined to make them as good as they could be.

But our last Christmas together was a difficult one indeed. My son had come to spend it with us, and Shirley had already explained to him that it wasn't going to be much of a Christmas with the way she was – both physically and emotionally – but we did our best to make it as enjoyable as possible.

Of course, I had no idea then that it would be the last we would share together.

So this year my son invited me to spend Christmas with them – a beautiful gesture and particularly poignant as I wasn't the only one who was grieving. This was to be his partner's first Christmas without her dad.

When I asked if she was sure she wanted me to be there, she simply replied that if it all got too much we could sit and weep in a corner together, which was a lovely thing to say. In the event, I think it worked as a good distraction for both of us.

But as seems to be the usual way of things, it was when I returned home that the tears really began to fall. I've thought a lot about why this should be, and I think it's a combination of no longer being surrounded by those I love, and walking back into an empty house that is bursting with memories. Whatever the reason, I wept as though I would never stop.

Naturally, now I have begun to tell people about the impending arrival of my grandson, they all leap on the news with gusto, wildly declaring how 'over the moon' I must be, and how good it is that I've got that to look forward to. It will, they say, give me a whole new focus to life, and I'm sure that all of these things are true. It is simply that I am so emotionally empty just now that I can't engage properly with the news. Not in the way that I would wish to.

And that is truly heartbreaking.

Chapter Thirty-Two
New Year malaise

3rd January 10:48

Here we are in the new year, it's 2024, and I seem to have sunk into a kind of a weird malaise. After what is nearly nine months now of filling the hours, of keeping myself as busy as I could, making sure that those hours between getting up in the morning and going to bed at night were full and busy – so that I didn't have to think too much, I suppose – I now find myself not wanting to do anything. I'll be quite happy sitting in the... sitting in the quiet, watching as I am now the rain hammering down outside, and not filling my hours with anything. Ever since Shirley died, I've had a problem of trying to motivate myself and get any kind of enthusiasm going for the things I used to enjoy doing, the things I have to do. But now the motivation, enthusiasm just seems to have gone completely. I've no interest, absolutely no interest in doing anything... and I'm just sitting... just sitting... just sitting.

*

I think I'm going through a bit of an existential crisis. I'm certainly not the person that I was, and this past year has without doubt changed me fundamentally. Like the caterpillar in its cocoon, I wait to see what I am changing into.

I remember that when I recorded this, I had begun to think that I was becoming one of those old people who will just sit in front the television for hours on end, while not necessarily taking in anything that they see. I remember my mother, towards the end of her life, doing precisely that, though in my mother's case the situation was exacerbated by her dementia and lack of physical mobility, which meant that the staff at her care home would wheel her into the lounge, sit her in front of the TV, and leave her there for, sometimes, quite long periods.

At least I could get up and move around, get on with some jobs, take the dog for a walk, make my meals – but there were still times when I sat in silence, letting the minutes slip by in a kind of haze. It feels odd to admit it, and I'm not sure it's entirely healthy, but I found such quiet immobility strangely comforting.

Chapter Thirty-Three
Covid Strikes!

5th January 07:45

It appears that now I have Covid, just on top of everything else. And… rather than feeling horrible, this raises one of the greatest worries that I've had since Shirley passed away, and that is being ill… being poorly on my own in the house, with no one to look after me or sort of run to the shops or anything like that. I've had various problems over the years… mostly with my back, but also with vertigo and things like that, where Shirley has been an absolute rock and has helped me so much, including things like… you know… helping me get to the toilet when I couldn't under my own steam, and now all that has gone. And that quite frankly terrifies me.

*

It is ironic that I managed to get through the 'Covid years' without contracting it, then succumb when it is all but over. I know, of course, that it *isn't* over, as my experience detailed above shows only too well, but it is long past its worst and now mostly presents as little more than a cold. In fact as I am writing this, current statistics say that one in four of us have it, though I don't know how they know, as testing seems to have pretty much gone out of the window.

Before Christmas I was really quite poorly with a cold and hacking cough, which took many weeks to get rid of. It was 'doing the rounds,' and I dutifully tested, thinking that the terrible cough indicated the likelihood of Covid. Negative. Just a horrible cold.

Then in January I had the tiniest of sniffles, hardly anything at all really, but I felt a bit achy, and knew I had some tests in the cupboard which were nearing their expiry date, so thought I'd do a test, never expecting in a million years that it would come out as positive. It did, and then took ten days of daily testing before a negative test finally signalled all was well.

I couldn't help thinking that Shirley would be standing over me saying "I told you so!" for throughout those Covid years she constantly told me that as I was the only one who was mixing with people, I would be the one to bring it into the house.

Not during the lockdowns, of course. No one mixed with anyone much back then.

Even doing the shopping was hardly a convivial experience, with the long socially distanced and masked queues snaking around the Co-op car park, waiting for the light over the door to turn green and admit the next lucky customer, who would then follow the one-way system through the aisles. That is, until we finally managed to get one of the rare as hen's teeth supermarket delivery slots, which negated the need to go out at all. The groceries would arrive at the door, the delivery man or woman standing back while we unloaded our order from the trays into our own bags, which we then took through into the kitchen where the stuff was dutifully wiped down with antiviral wipes before finally being stashed into the cupboards, fridge, and freezer.

Looking back, what an extraordinarily strange time it was.

Yet in a weird sort of way we quite enjoyed the first lockdown – Shirley was in a 'vulnerable' category, so was effectively shielding, and that meant staying home except when enjoying our allotted daily hour of exercise (making sure we didn't interact with anyone on the way, of course) – and for all the anxiety, the horror stories on the news, and the ever-increasing statistics of excess deaths, the fact that neither of us could work meant we were together 24/7, and that was truly lovely.

Chapter Thirty-Four
A really tough day

5th January 14:01

This is a really, really difficult day. I don't know why… obviously I'm feeling very low because of the Covid situation, but… but I'm just very, very low indeed. I just keep thinking that I'm not going to be able to get through this, I can't… I can't see a way through, I don't know how I can manage without Shirley. I don't know how I can continue on. It's really, really hard. And I just keep bursting into tears and wishing she was with me.

It's a really, really tough day today. Really, really tough.

*

I happened to catch the booker prize winning author of 'Prophet Song,' Paul Lynch, talking about his novel on Al Jazeera.[20] It was an interesting interview, but one line stood out to me. He said, "Grief is loss which is unrecoverable."

I think it chimed so perfectly with me because when I left Shirley all those years ago, there remained a subliminal thought that perhaps we might find each other again. I didn't realise that at the time, of course, being firmly of the belief that I had lost her forever, especially when the news came that she was getting married. As it happened, there were a couple of moments in the intervening years when our paths crossed, but the time wasn't right for us – not then – and we quickly returned to our separate lives.

Looking back on it now, I can see that there was, in a nebulous, unformed way, the whisper of a hope that at some time in the future I might be able to make reparation, to make good that terrible mistake – a mistake for which I had been consumed by guilt for the best part of thirty years.

Then, in 2010, the stars aligned and it happened. Both separated from our former partners, and with divorces pending, we were finally able to get back together.

And now, after thirteen wonderful years, she is gone, and I have failed her again. This time there is no hope of making recompense, and whatever mistakes I feel I made over her final few months can never be put right. So I drown in a sea of regret, held beneath the waves by the sheer weight of the should'ves, could'ves, and what ifs.

"Grief is loss which is unrecoverable."

Boy, oh boy, Paul Lynch… you can say that again.

Chapter Thirty-Five
Catharsis

7th January 08:11

It is eight o'clock in the morning, and I have just woken up. This is extraordinary because I never sleep this long. But it's an extraordinary morning for another reason as well, and that is for the first time I have had a proper dream about Shirley. I've said before that I haven't been dreaming about her, apart from the occasional little snippet in which she might appear briefly in a dream that wasn't about her. But last night I had a proper, proper dream about Shirley. I held her, I kissed her, we spoke about her suicide. She berated me for being upset… and yet the thing that most hit me about the dream was the fact that she seemed so at peace and content. She… I don't know, I find it very difficult to explain exactly how she was, but it was like… I don't know, there was a happiness about her, and for the first time I could actually appreciate… I could actually appreciate the fact that she was at peace. And this has made me feel… I don't know, it's been very cathartic… it's been a cathartic experience to have that dream. We just, as I say, hugged, and kissed, and talked… and then she went off to have a bath. I suppose the bath itself is… I don't know, what's the word? A… symbol of what happened. But… but there was such an air of peace, and content… and relief, in a sense, about her… that… that my overriding feeling now is that she has perhaps reached out to me in that dream to tell me that it's all okay. That she's happy and at peace.

The ... I don't know where the dream was set. It wasn't in our home here. It felt like it was in a flat. And now I think about it, perhaps... perhaps it harks back to the flat that we had together when we were first together in the 1980's, before I stupidly let her go... and... and... doomed myself to thirty years almost of let's say, less than happy relationships. Which is an understatement. So perhaps... perhaps, yes, it harks back to that. But as I lie here now, even though I am... even though I am... somewhat upset, I... I am feeling strangely at peace with myself. I have been so waiting for a dream like that, and it has finally arrived... and I am so grateful for it. As I say, cathartic.

*

I have heard many stories from people who say that their deceased loved ones have appeared to them in their waking hours, and many more who have spoken about being visited in dreams. As for the former, well, I had the peculiar experience during my university days of living in a house with a benign but nonetheless quite active supernatural resident, so I know that there may well be some truth in such reports, but wherever Shirley may be now, I like to think that she's got better things to do than to keep checking in on how I'm doing – and anyway, such appearances are traditionally interpreted as a sign of a restless spirit, and that's the last thing I would want Shirley to be.

But the idea of being visited in a dream is much more palatable – and has strong biblical resonances – so I am far more comfortable with that as a concept. And whether or not there is anything in it, or indeed whether it is merely the brain's way of processing the trauma of what has happened (see 'coda to Catharsis' below), I can honestly say that I welcomed the experience. You cannot know how comforting, how beautiful it is to be with your lost loved one again, even if only in a dream.

*

Coda to 'Catharsis'

I thought it would be worth also recording on here that I had the dream about Shirley – well I woke up about five o'clock this morning having had that dream – I then lay awake a little while thinking about it… and… I dunno, basking in a sort of a warm glow, I suppose, from having been close to her again. But when I went back to sleep, I then had a dream which included my father, who I also never dream about... and who died when I was twelve. And it took me a long time to grieve for my dad because I was thrust into the role of 'man of the house' and I had to do all the stiff upper lip stuff and look after my mum and stuff like that so… interesting that in the same night I had a proper dream about Shirley and *a dream about my dad. My brain is obviously doing something to process the whole thing around death. Anyway, I just thought it was worth recording that as well.*

Chapter Thirty-Six
Aftermath

7th January 11:36

There has been an unwelcome aftermath to the catharsis that I was speaking of earlier. And when… as I said, when I woke from my dream of Shirley that was probably the first time I'd felt anything approaching real happiness since she passed away. Then I went back to sleep and woke up I still had a feeling of moderate wellbeing from the aftermath of the dream although I was also quite upset, and that sadness, that upset, that grief, has just continued to pile on throughout the morning… just the sheer… the sheer knowledge of my loss has come tumbling back in, in many ways made worse by the fact that I had that small, lovely glimpse of what it was like when I was with her… and now she's no longer here… so in many ways what was a real blessing has turned out to be… well… I'm not going to say a curse, because it wasn't a curse. But it's turned out to have a most unwelcome effect.

*

Listening to this, I feel I have to file it under the heading 'memories: why I avoid them'. I have had great problems with memories because I find them too upsetting to dwell upon. This is exacerbated by well-meaning friends who, from the best of intentions, say things like "At least you have your memories" and "You have all those years of being together to look back on." The truth is, as I've said, that I can't bring myself to think about the times we had, simply because they are both too beautiful, and too painful, to dwell upon.

I'm aware that must sound strange to many of you, and I know lots of bereaved people for whom memories are quite literally a lifeline, but that is not my experience – not at the moment, at any rate – and as I have said countless times throughout this book, grief is a purely subjective thing, and all I can speak about with any certainty is the way that it has taken me. I sincerely hope that there *will* come a time when I can look back and feel warmth and comfort from those memories, but even now, more than a year after the event, that time still feels like it's a long, long way off.

Chapter Thirty-Seven
Turning a corner?

18th January 13:57

We are almost two-thirds of the way through January, and so far it's not been a bad month. I've had a lot of work on, so that has really helped, and... and I've been away from home quite a bit, which... which also in a weird way helps, because I'm not surrounded by all the memories and everything else that can be quite upsetting at times. So yes, so it's been a good month, and I was feeling like I'd probably turned a corner in this grief journey of mine. So driving back today... driving back from Surrey, I had decided that I would try and start to address what to do with Shirley's things. I had thought that perhaps shoes were the easiest things to... to get rid of first – pack them up, take them to the charity shop – but even as I thought about that, even as I thought about getting rid of her shoes, this wave of grief just hit me. It's all just bound up with what I've lost, and I don't know if I'm gonna to be able to do it now. So from being excessively positive and really thinking that I was getting somewhere, I kind of feel like I've plummeted back down to stage one. I know there'll be a lot of this, but... it's... it's just taken me I dunno... it's just taken me by surprise really, and I'm suddenly very, very down again.

*

I have known people who were off to the charity shop with their spouse's clothes almost as soon as the funeral was over, either because it was simply too painful to remain surrounded by their things, or because they felt the need to grasp the initiative and get on with their new solo life while still anaesthetised by the whirlwind of busyness that overwhelms us immediately following a death. (There are also, of course, those poor souls for whom their spouse's death represents a liberation from a loveless – or worse, abusive – marriage, in which case the immediate dumping of their partner's possessions is entirely understandable.)

I am not one of those people. Yes, I am reminded of Shirley every time I walk past her bobble-hat in the hall, or her dressing gown hanging on the side of the wardrobe; her coat on the back of the door or her make-up bag in the bathroom, but without those things the house would feel even more empty and bare than it already does.

Naturally, there have been some things that I have had to move around, and others that I have had to put away, but as I sit here now, more than a year has passed since her death, and all I have managed to get rid of have been her unused medications (returned to the pharmacy for safe disposal) and several pairs of spectacles (donated to a charity which can make use of them).

Drastic though it may seem, I have considered moving, which amongst other things would give me the impetus to dispose of a lot of stuff, as I would be setting up a new home just for me, and it wouldn't harbour any memories – other than the ones I might choose to take with me, photos and the like – but I suspect that even then I would find it difficult to let go, and would end up taking a lot of Shirley's things with me, possibly even replicating parts of our current home in the new environment.

There has been a lot of speculation amongst family and friends as to whether I would move away, and I have done a great deal of soul-searching about it. I am touched by the amount of people who have said they wouldn't want me to go – and the fact I have such a strong support network here and wonderful neighbours is worth its weight in gold – but just because people want me to stay is not in itself a good enough reason to do so. The essential problem of being in a place where every move or turn of the head brings me face-to-face with a memory remains, and many of those memories are like a knife through my heart.

So as with many of the decisions I've been faced with over this terrible time, I really don't know what to do – and making lists of pros and cons hasn't helped at all. Of course, the Catch-22 of the situation is that the main reason for my wanting to move – that is, if I stay, I remain surrounded by memories – is precisely the same reason for my *not* wanting to move, and that's a conundrum I can't easily solve.

After the initial rush of euphoria when we moved here, Shirley found it hard to settle. I'm not entirely sure why, or even whether there *was* an overriding reason, but she just didn't feel at home, and we had talked seriously about moving before Covid – and then her illness – put such plans on the back burner. But we never had much of an idea as to where we would like to go, and now I am on my own I am no nearer to knowing.

I am fortunate in that I have friends spread all around the country so wherever I might go I could be within striking distance of someone I know, and my son is keen for me to move closer to them, which is lovely, but I remain unsure. Hopefully I will have a lightbulb moment one way or another, but in the meantime I stay put, maintain the status quo, and soldier on.

Chapter Thirty-Eight
Another little milestone

21st January 11:44

Last night I got in late from a job… and I was still fairly kind of hyped up after the job, so couldn't go straight to sleep, so decided I would attempt to read in bed for a while. This may not sound like much, but I haven't been able to read in bed since Shirley died… 'cos it was something that we used to do together, always… go to bed, sit and read… sit in bed and read… and then turn the light out, have a little cuddle before we went to sleep. I haven't been able to bring myself to do it since, as I say… I've always made sure I'm really tired, then I just go straight to bed, turn the light out and go to sleep. But last night, as I say, I took a mug of hot chocolate and went to bed and read for half an hour. And the very fact that I was able to do that, without feeling terrible about it, without feeling upset, was in itself quite a little milestone.

*

After such a long time of having the concentration span of a gnat (not a scientific observation – for all I know gnats may have extraordinary concentration skills – but you know what I mean) I am so grateful that I can now read again. Over the last decade I have been trying to establish myself as a writer – with a modicum of success – but Shirley's death scuppered both my writing and my ability to read anything other than essential correspondence.

So reading *at all* is a major step forward, and being able to read in bed is even more significant (though at time of writing, that night remains the only time I have managed it). Shirley was herself an avid reader, consuming books both on her Kindle and in physical form, often reading four or five in a month. This meant that she was the perfect person to read and critique my own work before sending it out to publishers (what is known in the trade as a beta reader). And although what I write is not her preferred genre, her comments were invaluable.

Yet another block added to the teetering Jenga tower of why I miss her so very, very much.

Chapter Thirty-Nine
Depression?

24th January 10:04

A quick observation. I... I obviously feel very, very low some days, and I've often wondered whether that is depression, or just low mood. I've done a depression score thing with the local mental health people and I came out round about half way. So about fifty percent on the scale toward depression. But I think one of the most telling things, since Christmas, really, has been that I've stopped showering every day. I used to shower every day without fail and continued to do that even after Shirley had gone. But since Christmas I found myself... not... just not showering every morning, and I think the thing that points me towards depression on that is that it's not that I'm not showering because I feel that I don't need to shower, I'm not showering because I can't be bothered to shower... and I think that's quite a telling thing. I just hope that this spiral downwards doesn't... doesn't continue, and I can kick myself back up out of that.

*

I feel I should point out straightaway that just because I wasn't showering, doesn't mean I wasn't keeping myself clean. I was having what my mother used to describe as 'a good wash' – face, hands, pits and bits – and showering every few days (particularly when my hair needed washing) rather than every day, as had previously been my habit. As much as anything, this slowdown in the number of showers had to do with me finding the action of cleaning the shower afterwards a real grind. When you're sharing a living space with someone else, such things really matter... when you're on your own, it's easy to let such things slide.

I can't say that I've ever really experienced depression, having always been an optimistic, happy-go-lucky sort of individual. A glass half full, darkest hour just before the dawn type of person. But this experience has certainly changed me, and I can't say I like the person I have been over these last months. Is this depression? I'm not sure. Even looking back over the way this last year has affected me, I can't say whether I have experienced outright depression, or just grief wearing a mask.

A few minutes after I recorded the piece above, I went on to record a further piece on the same subject.

*

Coda to 'Depression?'

Further to the note I've just recorded about depression. Another indicator of this is that... whereas I've said many times that if it wasn't for my little dog, I would be quite happy with staying in bed all day when I have... when I think I have nothing to get up for. Being in bed is a safe haven. But because I have my little dog, I have always been getting up round about seven... well, between seven and seven-thirty... to let him out, because he's obviously been in his crate all night and he needs a wee. But that's started to slip... I've started to push that, which is, you know, not fair on him apart from anything else, but it's now often after eight o'clock when I get up and let him out... and then go back to bed, and... quite often I will be still in my dressing gown ten, ten-thirty, eleven o'clock, before I get myself together and take him out for his first proper walk. Once again, I think this is an indication that maybe a form of depression is starting to take hold.

*

Before the animal rights people hammer on my door, I should say that this state of affairs did not last very long, as I quickly realised that if I continued down this road I really would be abandoning hope. And it wasn't as if I was neglecting Barney – an extra half-hour in his crate of a morning (an hour at the most) was all it amounted to – but as I say in the recording, I noted it as indicative of my state of mind, and because I was aware of it, I was able to try to do something about it before it really took hold. I remember only too vividly watching Shirley steadily falling victim to depression as her pain grew worse – a relentless process that sucked the life out of her day by day – and try as I might, nothing I could do was of the slightest help.

She once told me that I would have to keep her 'up' because she couldn't do it for herself, and I tried so hard – always trying to be optimistic, encouraging her to look on the bright side, forever pointing to the next consultant appointment as the one which might offer a breakthrough – but to no avail. I was powerless against an enemy that gnawed at her soul until there was nothing left. One of her consultants told her that no matter how bad things seemed, she should try to concentrate on the positives, but I think that by that stage she had lost the fight… and shortly after, she was dead.

That is why I am loathe to call what I was experiencing depression, not in the worst extremes of the word anyway. I have seen what depression is, and what it can do, and I have swerved away from it.

Which makes me one of the lucky ones.

Chapter Forty
Another precious dream

26th January 07:15

I woke this morning from another lovely dream about Shirley. We were at a… or rather we were going to a birthday party… on a council estate, something to do with my magic club. We parked the car on a one-way street, and once I'd parked and got out of the… out of the car, which in my dream had then become a motorbike but you know how these things are, I walked back along the… back along the road with a little pussycat that was following me. I also for some reason had a long, Gandalf-style… staff, but again, who knows where that comes from in a dream. So I was striding along with this little… little ginger pussycat running alongside me, and couldn't see Shirley anywhere and I didn't know where I was going because I didn't have the address, but luckily I saw a couple of people that I recognised and so I followed them into the house where the party was, and Shirley was in there… she was… she was helping to set things up and we took the stuff out of the… out of the bag that we'd brought and – cheese and scones and pate and bread – and we were putting it on the table with the rest of the stuff… a couple of bottles of wine, but… but I'd left the beers in the boot of the car – ha! which had become a motorbike, but we won't go there! – and… and I'd got a couple of birthday cards, and I was showing Shirley and she was… she was advising me which one that I should… that we should write. And… and it was lovely… and it was just lovely, and we were together, and it was beautiful. And then… and then suddenly I said to her: 'How can you be here because you're dead? How can you be here because you're dead?' And she looked at me with that beautiful, beautiful smile of hers and she said: 'Don't you prefer this way? Don't you prefer this to me not being with you at all?' 'Cos I knew it was in a dream, and she was basically saying to me, 'well, don't you prefer being with me in dreams rather than me not being here at all?' which is of course what it had been because I hadn't dreamt about her for a very long… for months and months after it happened, and do you know? I DO prefer it. I do prefer it. It's lovely seeing her in the dream… it's lovely seeing her in my dreams. It's lovely, lovely, lovely having that time with her. So, yeah… I do prefer it. And I'm very, very grateful to her for coming to me in my dreams, even though when I wake up I realise she's no longer with me… it makes me cry… it makes me weep with longing. As I'm doing now. So it's a very bittersweet thing… but yes, please, Shirley… always come to me in my dreams. Always, always come to me in my dreams. Because I miss you so much…

*

Of all the recordings, this is perhaps the hardest one to listen back to. It is so raw with emotion, so desperate, and I can hardly get the words out for the tears that are strangling my voice. And I was in such distress when I woke, my whole body aching – no, *screaming* – with the loss, yet also profoundly grateful that I had been with her again, that she had come to me in this way.

I remember one of Shirley's consultants saying that there is so much about the brain we don't understand – an all-too-obvious statement, really, but in these days when we think the doctors and scientists know everything and can cure just about anything, it is a salutary thing to reflect on. He was speaking about whatever neurological disorder might have been causing Shirley's symptoms and concluded by saying that in cases such as hers, it is often impossible to find a cause – which may be true, but wasn't very helpful.

Yet in the case of dreams, our subconscious holds sway, granting us these glimpses of heaven and hell without fear or favour.

"Your young men will see visions and your old men shall dream dreams"[21]

It is little wonder that dreams and visions feature in just about every world religion. They are powerful stuff.

It's also worth noting here that I was accompanied for part of this dream by a ginger cat, as throughout my childhood I grew up with a ginger cat (called, with great imaginative flair, 'Ginger') who was very much 'my' cat, having been brought into the household at about the same time as I was, and who lived to the ripe old age of eighteen. I felt his loss keenly, so once again, it is interesting the way your subconscious brings these things back to you through your dreams.

While we are reflecting on the workings of the brain, I can't recommend highly enough a book called 'The Grieving Brain' by the American neuroscientist Mary-Frances O'Connor.[22]

If, like me, you want to understand what is going on in your brain when you are grieving, and why it has to happen, this book will fundamentally change the way you see grief and grieving, while by no means invalidating your own lived experience. Yes, it is an academic work, but it is so well written that it's accessible to anyone with a thirst to know what's going on. As well as explaining the research that's been done to date, she talks about many of the phenomena that you will experience while grieving (including many that I have experienced myself and described in these recordings) and provides much-needed assurances that those experiences are normal and that, contrary to what you may be feeling, you are NOT going mad.

I have found it phenomenally helpful.

Chapter Forty-One
Dusting

27th January 14:31

Today has seen the extraordinary spectacle of me going round the house with a duster… with tears rolling down my cheeks. The problem is that, as I think I've said before, I haven't been able to work up the courage to get rid of any of Shirley's things yet, so here we are, over nine months in, and things are still pretty much where she's left them. I'm just so aware that if I start getting rid of them, not only does it feel like expunging what remains of her from my life, but… but also it means that the house will be very empty – all those shelves and hooks and goodness knows what will be empty – and the place will feel awful. So… so when I'm dusting, I'm obviously confronted even more than usual with all of these things because I have to… I have to dust them, I have to dust round them, I have to move them in order to dust, I have put… I have to put them back, I mean, all the photos and everything else… it's just… it's just difficult. And today, I just found it really, really hard.

You'll be pleased to know that I did manage to complete the dusting.

*

I still find dusting very difficult, emotionally. Not only for the reasons expressed in the recording, but also because Shirley was very house-proud and used to vacuum and dust every day. I don't, and so feel like I am letting her down when I notice the dust accumulating, and that just piles on further guilt. My counsellor talks about 'reframing' such experiences, so that instead of feeling guilt for *not* doing it, I should turn it into a positive so that whenever I *do* do it, I am doing something that Shirley would have been proud of me for, and to find comfort in that.

I can see where he's coming from. Generally, I find it difficult to see how grief can be reframed into a positive, but I guess that individual aspects of it such as this can be – and realising that is quite a step forward, I suppose.

It's the photos that are the worst though, as I still can't look back on our memories without bursting into tears. One of the many awful things about grief is that it is a wound that you can't see, so you have no physical indication of how it is healing, unlike a wound on the surface where you can follow its progress as it heals. Yet the wound is no less real, and no less painful, than if you had plunged a knife into your chest, and just as salt rubbed into that physical wound would increase the pain significantly, so the pictures force me to remember, and that's hard. But as I've said before, I wouldn't be without them, and I still trust that in time I'll be able to look at them with the fond glow of loving remembrance, rather than through the burning eyes of grief.

.

Chapter Forty-Two
A candle in the church

4th February 13:53

I am sitting in our parish church of St. Mary, having just lit a candle for Shirley. I'm looking up at a large stained-glass window of Jesus, his feet on the world. Barney led me here today, actually. He knows the way well now, because coming here and lighting a candle has been a source of comfort all the way through this dreadful, dreadful time. Now when we go on a walk and we come anywhere close to the church Barney always leads me in. But today we weren't intending to come here at all… and he just looped around so that we would come here. And as I sat, just reflecting, quietly, on everything… a shaft of light came in through the side windows… and it was like a message, a message of peace… and that's rather lovely.

*

Back in chapter thirteen, I mentioned how, since Shirley's death, I have struggled with some aspects of the Christian faith, most specifically the question 'why does God allow so much suffering in the world?' To those of a theological bent there *are* answers of course, but at times like these they can come across as patronising platitudes. What answers can there possibly be for a parent who has lost a child, or for anyone whose family has been torn apart by the savagery of war? At such times there can *be* no words, just basic human compassion for a fellow soul in torment.

Yet despite my struggles with what it *means* to have Faith, amplified to the nth degree by my current circumstances, I have never failed to find peace and solace in simply sitting in a quiet church, reflecting on the beauty that is to be found in solitude, and feeling the weight of history perching lightly upon my shoulders. How many people, I always wonder, have sat just as I am sitting now – staring up at the beautiful colours of the stained glass – and felt the indefinable presence of something beyond our understanding?

Since I properly embraced Christianity in my late teens, drawn by the message of love and peace and care for others that sits at the very heart of the gospel – and cemented by an intensely personal experience of the power of the Holy Spirit – I have always felt that God was with me, even in those times when *I* turned my back on *Him*. (I use the male pronoun here because that is traditional within the church – the image of God the father – though I suspect that gender is not something that applies in this context, actually.)

But when Shirley died I couldn't find God anywhere, and for the first time I felt truly abandoned. Christianity is by its very nature a joyful, celebratory religion, with Easter the greatest celebration of all. Yet because my grief is now so intimately linked to the Easter period, I can no longer feel the joy encapsulated in the festival – indeed, this year I actively avoided it – and that fuels my guilt even more.

As the minister at Shirley's celebration service said, the fact that Shirley died at Easter should give us a joyful hope in the resurrection and the promise of eternal life. It *should*, and prior to Shirley's death it would have, but right now I struggle to experience that joy. In so many ways I felt (and still feel, to a certain extent) the embodiment of the old saying that it is easy to be a Christian when all is going well; the crunch comes when your life falls apart. And I was seriously floundering.

RS Thomas, in his poem 'In Church' has the following lines, lines which seem to echo much of what was going on for me at that time:

"There is no other sound
In the darkness but the sound of a man
Breathing, testing his faith
On emptiness, nailing his questions
One by one to an untenanted cross."[24]

In Christian mysticism, there is the concept of 'the dark night of the soul,' and that absolutely describes what I feel I'm going through. Yet I am heartened by the fact that every book I have read from Christian authors recounting their own personal journey through grief and bereavement shows them to have had the same or similar experience. Even such a seminal Christian author as C.S.Lewis[6] felt utterly abandoned. And that gives me great hope.

However, as days turned to weeks and weeks to months, I began to see signs that He *was* still there, even though I could no longer *feel* His presence.

And the fact that a simple shaft of light could change my perspective is a sign that somewhere in all of this, somewhere deep below the surface, healing *is* happening. But as I have said before, I suspect it's going to be a long, hard road.

Chapter Forty-Three
The birthday

7th February 23:15

Today has been another difficult day, of which I have several coming up. Today was Shirley's birthday, and… I have spent a great deal of it in… tears, for various reasons. Firstly, I… bought Shirley a book for her birthday. Sounds silly, doesn't it? But… it was a book that… that she knew was being written and that she really wanted… Noel Fitzpatrick's latest book 'Keira and Me'. It arrived… a week ago and I… put it away, so she couldn't see it before her birthday. Ridiculous, isn't it? But I… I kind of decided to myself that I was going to spend today reading that book on her behalf, because I know how much she would have loved to have read it. I've… over the years I've bought her all of the books that he's… that he's written, and she really… she really likes him, she really likes… likes the books. So first of all I wished her happy birthday this morning when I woke up, and I… got the book out and showed her, that is to say I showed it to the picture of her in my bedroom which is one of the pictures that I talk to all the time, and that upset me. I got quite upset about showing her the book that she was never going to be able to read.

But then, of course there was the Facebook messages… I have to say that there weren't many… well, weren't any, in fact… wishing her specifically happy birthday, which was a good thing because at least that means that I've managed to get the… word out to everybody… that she had passed away. But there were lots and lots of messages of condolence to me...and that... and that had me in floods of tears again. And those messages kept coming in all through the... all through the day, so every time I checked Facebook there was another reason for me to burst into tears.

Then of course, I... sat down to read the book, and the book was absolutely nothing like I was expecting, although it was far, far better than anything I could have imagined. Rather than the normal autobiographical writings which his other books have been, this was just the most beautiful pean... poem to the love that existed between him and his little dog Keira, and the profound and awful loss when... she finally passed away. A book about love and loss... beautifully, beautifully illustrated... a very simple, easy read... I read through it in about, well, less than an hour, but... I had to stop every couple of minutes to wipe the tears from my eyes because it was such a beautiful, beautiful book – and beautifully produced, too, I mean, just... just a phenomenally lovely book, one of the best, the most beautiful books I've read in a long time, and it really, really spoke to me, really pulled at my heartstrings, and I was in floods of tears throughout the entire experience of reading it.

Then, of course, some friends put a card, a 'thinking of you' card through the letterbox this afternoon so that again set me off. And then this evening I was due to go out for a meal with some very, very good friends who have been absolute stalwarts and supported me throughout this entire awful, awful experience, and just as I was going out the door a... delivery van drew up with some flowers from my lovely... daughter-in-law to be... and my son. So once again I just looked at the flowers and burst into tears, so all through the day everything has conspired to make sure that my cheeks remained wet. However, I've got to the end of it... got to the end of the day, and... yeah, it's been an interesting one.

*

Everyone will tell you that the first set of anniversaries are the hardest – which has to be one of the most obvious bits of information that you will ever be told. Yet you do have to think about how you are going to manage them. Somehow you need to map a path through these dates that glare threateningly at you from the pages of the calendar.

For me, I cope by making sure all my plans are in place well in advance. I know this strategy won't suit everyone, but I find it easiest to have a structured day so I can see how I'm going to get from the start to the finish line, as it were. This is how I have got through the last year and a bit, by putting one foot in front of the other and filling my days – and I've found this doubly important for the 'special' days; days when I know that grief will explode around me like a thunderclap.

My birthday I filled with work – so I was surrounded by people all day, with plenty to occupy my thoughts – then treated myself to a Chinese meal in the evening; Christmas was spent with my son and his fiancée (not that she was officially his fiancée then, but I knew that a proposal was imminent...); New Year's Eve I spent with friends.

So, I fill the days with busyness and try to avoid surprises that will drag me down, though on this occasion, as I say in the recording, there was a succession of somewhat unexpected events that had me in tears. So much for the strategy…

To quote Robert Burns: "The best laid schemes o' mice an' men / Gang aft a-gley…"[25]

You can say that again, Rabbie old chum.

Chapter Forty-Four
Positivity

15th February 11:43

I've been told that instead of just recording… entries when I'm feeling particularly down, I should also record a few positive ones on here, so… hopefully this will be one of those. I'm not feeling bad at all today, in fact I'm feeling more positive than I have in a very long while. I don't know why that is particularly today, although yesterday was Valentine's Day and I was expecting that to be a really bad day, and in fact it wasn't too bad at all. I managed to get through it with only a few little… little feelings of… of upset here and there, but I actually didn't burst into tears at any point during the day, which is a great… a great improvement on… the previous Wednesday which was, of course, Shirley's birthday, and I was in tears the entire flamin' day, so… so yes, that was a great improvement yesterday… helped I think by the fact that Open Door rang me in the morning to check on how I was feeling and that… and that helped an awful lot, as it always does. I'm very, very grateful to them for having stuck with me and seen me through this entire… difficulty. So, yes… so today I'm not feeling bad at all. That's no guarantee of course that tomorrow isn't gonna be another downer, but at the moment… I'm feeling pretty positive, and I'm getting on with things in a positive mind frame. So, there you go… I've recorded it now, for all those people who say I should record positive stuff. There it is.

*

Almost as soon as I had recorded this, the postman delivered a belated birthday card for Shirley, and my positive mood cracked apart. It had come from a good friend and ex-colleague and contained a great deal of chatty, catch-up news which eloquently spoke to the fact that this dear, lovely person had no idea that Shirley was no longer alive to read her words. As my eyes scanned the flowing lines, all the feelings that had assailed me on her actual birthday struck like a tsunami. But now there was a further reason for my tears, for I thought I had been scrupulous in contacting all her friends, and everyone else who needed to know, yet here I was confronted by the evidence of my failure.

And my catalogue of failures is what haunts me most.

Since that first terrible night, I had been struggling with the knowledge that I had failed her. I do not berate myself on a practical level – in that regard I had done everything I possibly could. I took over all the housework, cooked all the meals, drove her everywhere she needed to go for hospital and consultant's appointments, held her when she needed to feel me close, and constantly reassured her that everything was going to be alright. And this last point was where the problem lay. As I said in chapter thirty-nine, as her health and her mood deteriorated, she told me that she was relying on me to keep her buoyed up, as she couldn't do it on her own – and I'm ashamed to say that I took her at her word. I stopped listening to her when she tried to tell me just how awful she felt, always countering by pointing to the next appointment; telling her that there was always hope; that the next consultant might provide the diagnosis that would lead to a breakthrough, that would mean we had turned a corner and she would be on the road to recovery. In short, it sent me into a spiral of denial.

In my misplaced determination to jolly her along and keep her positive, I failed to take on board just how bad things had become, and failed to be empathetic when she needed that more than anything.

Most of all, though, I failed to stop her taking her life. And for that I will never be able to forgive myself.

Chapter Forty-Five
A mediterranean dream

18th February 07:50

Okay, so last night I had another dream. This one was… set in some mediterranean… or maybe North African town, and I was driving into an underground car park which apparently had been… or seemingly had been carved out of the rock. I was with a couple of people; I've got no idea who they are… but once we'd parked up, we went to a sort of a little… I don't know… it was a strange little… little kind of sink thing set into the wall and we seemed to be, I don't know, doing the washing-up or something which was bizarre but there you go, it's a dream… but I was talking about Shirley, and about my other marriages… and… and basically I was telling this person that… that Shirley was the one, and that people spend their whole lives looking for the one, and I had her… I found her very… very early in my life, and then threw her away. But I didn't feel any sadness about telling them, I felt a great feeling of… of happiness and peace that I could pass that on to others… that… that… that… I don't know how to put it… the fact that I had found my one… and even after my ridiculous act of… of throwing her away, we managed to find each other again and have thirteen lovely years. It was a positive and happy thing to speak about and I'm glad that I was able to do that in my dream.

*

A bit of a garbled recording, this, but significant on several levels.

Firstly, the setting. Shirley and I had, during that initial couple of years we had together, taken a wonderful holiday together in Tunisia – a holiday that was booked on the spur of the moment, and was always, and still is, an extraordinarily precious memory. The trip included a visit to the cave dwellers of Matmata, which I guess is where the imagery in my dream came from.

When I was going through Shirley's things, I found the set of slides that we had taken on that trip, which she had lovingly kept all these years, a testament to what that holiday had meant to her too.

And therein lies the significance.

Up until this point, I had been unable to revisit *any* of our memories without bursting into tears, so to bring back this one now felt like my dream was telling me that it was okay to look back on fond memories, like I was giving myself permission. And that is the overriding feeling that remained with me upon waking.

Secondly, I was speaking within the dream about my catastrophic decision to finish the relationship. To say I was afraid of commitment at that stage in my life would be an understatement, as I had already been engaged twice before Shirley and I got together, and each time I had blown the relationship out of the water. As I have said before, I was young and stupid, but that is no excuse for the cavalier way I lived life throughout my late teens and early twenties. In retrospect, I am ashamed of the person I was back then; hate the way I moved almost seamlessly from one relationship to another with no thought of the emotional wreckage I might have left in my wake.

But when it happened with Shirley, I immediately had the deep-rooted conviction that this was one too many, a break-up too far. And even though I justified it to myself endlessly, I know within my heart that I was just wrong. Shirley used to say that had we remained together then, we might not have stayed the course, and maybe that's true, but I think she was just being magnanimous. I know that in so many ways, that decision destroyed our lives, and I was the luckiest man in the world to have been given the chance to make amends, and finally create the life together that we should have had all those years ago.

Regrets, again. So very many regrets.

Chapter Forty-Six
Another day, another bereavement course

29th February 15:19

This morning was the second one of the… new bereavement course that I'm on, and it was very tough, it was very challenging. Apart from other things we had to… reflect upon what happened around the death… how we felt, how… you know, it was just very difficult. I don't need the time to reflect because I live with it every moment of every day, it's always there with me. So… I felt quite…quite panicky really, about it, and… I was due to be going out for lunch after the course which I did, but… but I had to make my apologies and duck out early because I was feeling in such a state, and even now I'm at home and sitting here I feel very… very nervy and on edge. So… so let's hope that… I mean, I knew the course was gonna be challenging… but let's hope it… it does some good as well as making me feel like a blubbering wreck.

*

This is the second online course that I have taken part in since losing Shirley. The first was the 'Facing the Future' course[10] of which I have spoken before, run by the Samaritans[11] and geared specifically towards survivors of bereavement by suicide. This one, however, was targeted at anyone who had been bereaved under any circumstances, and was run by Steps 2 Wellbeing[26], a Dorset mental health initiative. The chief difference between the two – aside from the subject matter – is that whereas the Samaritans' course was unstructured and aimed to bring together people with similar experiences just to talk and support each other, this one had a much more formal structure, right down to the fact that it was accompanied by a workbook. Looking through the workbook in advance of the session, I instantly knew that this would be a difficult day.

And so it proved.

I guess the idea was to deal with any feelings of avoidance or denial by forcing us to confront the details of our loved one's death – but for me, all it did was bring on a dreadful crippling anxiety around having to speak about it in front of the group. So I said nothing, just sat before my computer screen in an extreme state of nervous panic.

I was far from alone, however. Of the thirteen participants, only three plucked up the courage to talk about their experience, and for that I heartily applaud them. In my job, I am used to the sensation of surging adrenaline that sends your stomach into knots and can ultimately result in crippling stage-fright, and have always been able to overcome it. But not today.

And the feeling persisted throughout the following week. Prior to this session, I had been feeling like I was finally getting somewhere with regards to my grief, but this really set me back, to the extent that once again I found myself teetering on the edge of tears for large swathes of the subsequent days.

For a course that is supposedly designed to help with the ravages of grief, this particular session did me absolutely no favours.

Chapter Forty-Seven
A message from WhatsApp

9th March 11:33

Several of my recordings on here have been about dreams, and… they've been lovely. I haven't had many dreams about Shirley but when I have, they've always been wonderful. Yesterday I got a WhatsApp message from her cousin who said that she'd been thinking about Shirley a lot recently and… and that night she had had a beautiful dream of her. She said it was so real… she looked radiant, she was wearing a beautiful white top with embroidered flowers, her hair was a little longer than it had been… and she said that she kept saying to Shirley how good she looked, and Shirley said "yes, I am really very very happy". And it… and it really affected her and… obviously was also very comforting. I read it with… well with a mixture of emotions really, but… the first thing that came to mind was a photo that I'd found at the bottom of a drawer… when I was going through some of Shirley's things. She'd never shown it to me, so I don't know when it was taken, or what the event was, or… or how it was… you know, just… how it came to be, but it was of Shirley in white, with flowers in her hair, streamers from her wrists, looking all the world like a… like a… young… woodland goddess or nature goddess… absolutely beautiful. When I found it, I couldn't stop looking at it. And… hearing about this dream… brought me straight to that picture. And it is lovely, and it is… it is beautiful to think that… that… if there is anything in appearances in dreams, that she is wanting to tell us that she's in a happy, happy place, and that makes me… well, that makes me feel good.

*

I recorded a piece about a very similar dream I had back in chapter thirty-four, and I found it intriguing that her cousin, who was perhaps the person Shirley was closest to after myself, had much the same dream. Obviously, there is a straightforward and rational explanation for this – her cousin admitted that she had been thinking about Shirley a lot, so it would be logical that she would pop up in her dreams – but it is nevertheless comforting to think that she might just be reaching out to us to let us know that she's okay.

And I am more than happy to see it that way.

A thread that runs throughout this book is just how difficult it can be to find anything positive in the all-pervading gloom of grief, but author and poet Donna Ashworth, in her wonderful poem 'Peace at Last'[27] ends with these lines, which resonate with me so strongly:

> "I hope you have found
> the *peace*
> you so sought here on earth
>
> the peace that outran you
> at every turn
> the peace that was never within your reach.
>
> Because you deserve that peace
> my love
> at long last.
>
> And I will try to take peace from that.
>
> I will try to take peace from that."

Chapter Forty-Eight
Another meltdown

19th March 11:35

So I've just had another total meltdown. We're coming up to the anniversary of Shirley's death and… I imagine that's got a lot to do with it because it's… it's just so… it's all coming back so fresh in my mind. But I'm so tired of letting people know… telling people that… that I'm okay, that I'm doing okay. It's so tiring having to keep up that façade all the time… and in fact here we are a year on and I'm still completely a mess, I'm still completely… just crying and crying and crying. I got a… email today from an organisation that's going to be providing me with face-to-face counselling. Everyone who's supported me so far has said that that's probably gonna be the best route for me now. I'm just waiting for a time and date when that can start. I just really hope, I really hope that they're gonna be able to help me get past this.

*

This is just another example of how grief can come out of nowhere and leave you howling on the floor. Listening back, I see I was trying to find the triggers – the upcoming anniversary, the email from the counselling service – but it still came out of the blue. I was preparing to go away for work, had just returned home from dropping Barney off at his dog-sitters, and was due to hit the road about half an hour later. So I was in full-on distraction mode with lots to occupy me both physically and mentally when BANG! the grief smacked me in the guts. On the recording you can hear that not only am I fighting back the tears – unsuccessfully, I might add – but also literally gasping for breath. And the desperation in my voice with that final sentence is the worst it has been since the very early days, yet this comes almost a year after the event.

Now, everything I have learned so far about grief – through the courses I have done and the books I have read – has in some measure prepared me for this and has assured me that there's nothing unusual about continuing to get these 'attacks.' In fact, it's not unusual to continue getting them for many years after the event, but I am told that they will decrease in frequency, and be much less debilitating, as time goes on, and I sincerely hope that will be the case.

I recently saw a meme on Facebook which said, in essence, that though it can be hard to begin another chapter of a book when you know that your favourite character will no longer be in it, nevertheless the story continues, and if you *don't* turn the page, you will never know what happens next. (The meme was much more poetically succinct than that, but that's what it meant.)

And this is the central tragedy of suicide, for the person who takes their own life is cutting off any chance of seeing how the story continues, any hope of experiencing what is to come. Of course, when you reach that level of despair where death seems the only option, then it becomes impossible to see *any* future, *any* glimmer of hope in the all consuming blackness.

I should have been able to give her that hope, and though I tried as hard as I could to convince her that together we would get through this – ultimately, I failed.

And I must live with that for the rest of my life.

Chapter Forty-Nine
Easter Saturday

30th March 07:34

I've just woken up in real distress... I've said so many times before that sleep is my refuge and I've had some... some lovely dreams about Shirley... well, this night, the one I've just woken up from, was just horrendous. I'd been at a party... well, we'd *been at a party. The people at the party kept changing and you know, like a dream, one minute I was there one minute I wasn't... and it... it was all kind of... there was something about trying to get groceries and all sorts of things mixed in there but the main thing about the dream was that we'd been at this party and we'd gone back to the car in the car park and discovered that we hadn't got... we hadn't got Barney's food and drink bowls, we'd left them there. And I remember seeing the woman from the party cradling them in her arms so... so Shirley said she'd go back and... at least I think it was Shirley, I'm getting really confused now... said that she would go back and get them. And she'd... she was gone a little while and came back and said that... she said that... she said that the woman had said that they'd searched around for them and couldn't find them anywhere, they weren't there. And I got very angry because I remembered seeing her with them, right at the end as we were leaving, so I went storming back in and... and turned the place upside down and couldn't find them anywhere. So I apologised to the people at the party and... and came back into the carpark and the car wasn't there. So I went down a... I went down there because the party was in like a block of flats and each flat had its own carpark on that level... so I went down a level to see if I'd come out at the wrong place but the car wasn't there either, so I went out into the... street and sat on a wall and started trying to phone Shirley but the phone wouldn't give me her number. I kept putting in 'S-H-' and it gave me all sorts of weird things, it kept connecting me to people that I didn't know or didn't need to speak to or... so I kept cutting it off and trying again and trying again and every time I put in the ... her name in, something else would come up. There was one point where it tried to connect me to my son which I guess, thinking about it logically, was kind of me reaching out to him in distress, because... because I was getting more and more frustrated and more and more angry and jabbing and jabbing into the phone and I just couldn't find Shirley anywhere and she wasn't there, she wasn't in the phone... and there was no way I could get in touch with her because the phone just wasn't giving me her number and... and I was just getting more and more angry and I was screaming at the phone and shouting and yelling and jabbing and jabbing and it just kept giving me... giving me other people, other numbers, other names, and... and I was on the verge of throwing the phone onto the... onto the ground, and... and that's when I woke up. So I woke up in this terrible... in this terrible distress of... of being desperate to contact her and I just couldn't, 'cos the phone wasn't letting me do it, and I was getting so angry and frustrated and... and that's the feeling I that had when I woke up... I was just in so much distress and I...*

[There now follows a 28 second pause in the recording.]

There is a weird irony to what has just happened. I came to stop this recording, and the phone itself had shut off... or rather, closed down, you know... so... so I had to start it up again and the phone was still recording... like the phone wouldn't let me shut it off. How weird is that?

*

There are several things to say about this recording. Firstly, as I have stated before, when it comes to the 'Stages of Grief,' I haven't really experienced any of them so far other than depression. Mary-Frances O'Connor[22] states that most clinicians no longer use this model – it has been superseded by more useful ways of looking at the grieving process that take into account that not everyone passes through all the five 'stages' and certainly not in a linear way. However, everyone acknowledges that anger is a very common stage, but it is one that I haven't experienced – up until this dream. I'm sure psychologists would have a field day interpreting that, but I'm just going to put it out there. Perhaps what we don't allow ourselves to show – or in my case don't even feel – in our waking lives will always find an outlet through our subconscious, like a safety valve in a hot water system.

The second thing to say is that I always knew the Easter weekend was going to be rough, forming as it does one of the anniversaries of Shirley's death (thank you, Christianity, for making Easter a moveable feast, giving me a 'double whammy' of anniversary dates to contend with) but I'd had my first counselling session with Suicide&Co[23] just two days earlier and felt pretty positive about being able to face it. So the result of this dream was to knock all that sideways. Luckily, I had arranged to go for a long dog walk with an understanding friend that afternoon – which worked wonders for my equilibrium – and then to go to stay with my son for a couple of days, so at least I knew that I wasn't going to be on my own very much over the actual holiday, for which I was very grateful.

Thirdly, it shows my subconscious howling in despair at the utter hopelessness of my position. In the dream I couldn't find her, had no idea where she was, and this just fuelled my anxiety, my need, and the desperation of my longing. She had been snatched away from me, and I had no way of tracking her down, or of finding her again; and while that is something that my conscious, logical mind has accepted, my subconscious mind reacts against it, railing against the heartless cruelty of the situation, and shakes its fist at the bleak, uncaring universe.

Finally, it underlines just how much I miss simply being in her company, having her with me, being able to talk to her and share the minutiae of life.

And that, perhaps, is the unkindest cut of all.

Chapter Fifty
A strange day – dreams, rain, & counselling

4th April 17:13

Today's been a very peculiar sort of day. It started off with me waking up from a horrible dream, in which I had… I had got rid of the van that… that I bought soon after Shirley died. And instantly in my dream I regretted getting rid of it and I desperately tried to find the garage that I'd sold it to, but it wasn't where… where it had been and I was running down streets and alleys and roads to try and desperately find this garage so that I could get the van back, 'cos the van meant so much to me, you know, as a memory of Shirley…it's all sort of bound up… but I couldn't find it anywhere and I was running round and round and round and getting more and more agitated and that's the… that's when I woke up, and… so that's the mood that I was in when I woke.

So I decided that I would take myself off in the van because it needs some new windscreen wipers, so I thought I would go to Halfords to get some. So I set off and then it started pouring with rain and the windscreen wipers weren't working, and I had to… I had to kind of bodge them up so they would work… got to Halfords and they hadn't got any… any windscreen wipers of the type I wanted so I then went to… went to another place that Halfords recommended… Eurospares I think it was called… and… and they hadn't got it either. So… so I came back feeling very sort of frustrated and ordered them online which I should have done in the first place.

So… so then I started to… to get very agitated. Took Barney out for a walk which… which calmed me down a little bit, and then I went into my counselling session. So…so when the counsellor asked me "how you feeling today?" I kind of had to say, "I don't know, really… it's just been a very peculiar day." The counselling session was very good, though. He's a nice guy and I get on with him well, and hopefully it's going to be helpful. But early days… early days.

*

When I told my counsellor about the dream, he instantly drew parallels with what I had told him the week before about my regretting leaving Shirley all those years ago, and I must admit as soon as he pointed it out it became as clear as day. Regretting getting rid of the van and then discovering there was no way to find it again is such an obvious mirroring that I can't believe I didn't see it myself.

This is part of the problem, though. Everything is so bound up with Shirley that moving forward while I am still physically bound to the things and places that we shared together feels like an impossibility. Not that I *want* to 'move on,' as Shirley will always be part of my life, but I have to find a way to function better than I am at the moment.

My counsellor is a great proponent of mindfulness and self-compassion and has given me several exercises and websites to help me, should I want to go down that road. Some – especially the American ones – are a bit too 'new-agey' for me, but I think there is a lot to be gained from mindfulness as a concept and a tool, and I intend to continue with those exercises that suit me. After all, I entered this process with the attitude that I was prepared to take any offers of help that I could get, and I do feel that that open-minded outlook has by and large paid dividends.

He also introduced me to the Mary-Frances O'Connor book, for which I am very grateful indeed. In fact, if that were to be the only thing I got out of counselling (and it isn't, by the way, it's been helpful in lots of ways), the sessions would have been worth it for that alone.

One of the most controversial things that has come out of my counselling sessions, and which was picked up again later (totally independently) by my therapist, is the idea that perhaps I subconsciously gave Shirley the space she needed to take ownership of her death. It is an intriguing idea, but one that I'm not at all sure about. Throughout counselling, I have grappled long and hard with the reason for my guilt, which arises for the most part from the fact that I am convinced I could have stopped her, if only I hadn't been in such deep denial that she could ever take such an action.

In his book 'The Way of Rest' Jeff Foster[28] says:

"You cannot save anyone. You can be present with them, offer your groundedness, your sanity, your peace. You can share your path with them, offer your perspective. But you cannot take away their pain."

I know now that this is all too true, but arriving at that understanding has been a bitter road to travel, strewn on every side with anguish and remorse.

People have told me that had I managed to stop her on that night, there is no guarantee she wouldn't have tried again the next, or the next, and that is true – ultimately you cannot stop someone from exercising their own free will – but though she had spoken several times of suicide as an escape from her interminable pain, she had assured me she would never be able to go through with it.

And I clung to that like a drowning man catching hold of a broken spar.

Chapter Fifty-One
Triple Whammy

7th April 15:03

This weekend has been a bit of a surprise. I've been telling everybody about my 'double whammy,' in that… because Shirley died at Easter and the date of Easter moves around it means that I have the… the Easter itself to cope with, followed by the actual date of her death. But of course, I've completely forgotten this weekend, because this weekend it is 52 weeks exactly since she died, so this Sunday, today, is the day of the anniversary, really. And it took me a bit by surprise and when I realised that I had a little bit of a meltdown… not as bad as it could have been, to be honest… but still, as I say, it took me by surprise. So… so whereas I've got stuff in… in hand, I've got things planned for the run up to, and indeed the day of the actual date of her death, and of course I had stuff in place for Easter… going up to my son's… so I, you know, had ways to cope with that, but this weekend I hadn't thought about at all so I'm having to navigate my way through it as… as best I can. So yeah, it came as a… bit of a surprise. Triple whammy eh? Brilliant.

*

As you know by now, I have largely got through this first year by organising my days, filling my hours with various tasks that I have no enthusiasm for, but which perform a necessary function – and as I recounted in chapter forty-eight, the other anniversaries and special days have all been programmed up to the hilt. So this one was a terrible oversight. I simply hadn't considered it until the morning of Saturday when I marked off another week on the calendar (I have been marking the weeks with short vertical lines in groups of four struck through on the fifth, like a prisoner scratching on their cell wall to mark the number of days since their incarceration began) and realised that this was the fifty-second week.

I was completely thrown by it and could feel the adrenaline flooding my veins, leading to a sudden rise in feelings of stress and panic. As always at these times, I reached for Barney's lead and whisked him out for a walk, which provided both an immediate distraction and the time and space to calm the savage waters.

Once back home, I concentrated on my 'to do' lists, and the weekend passed in a flurry of activity, though I did manage to dedicate some time to Shirley. Time to sit quietly, to tearfully register the significance of the day, and to mourn.

It is also worth noting that I made myself a shepherd's pie for Sunday dinner. My favourite meal since I was very young, it provided the comfort I needed to restore a sense of balance to an otherwise difficult couple of days.

As I have said many times before… it's whatever works for you.

Chapter Fifty-Two
Ink

10th April 13:24

So here we are at the third, and thankfully last, of the three anniversary days for Shirley's death. I had promised myself that I would get a celebration tattoo... to... to commemorate her life and... and basically that's what I went along and did this morning. I got myself a little bit worked up about it before I went because I didn't really know what to expect having never had a tattoo before... but... but the guy was just so helpful and put me at ease and it was actually a really nice experience... a really good experience... so... so I now have my tattoo and... and that will obviously be with me forever. On the way back I picked up a bit of special food for tonight so that I can have a little... a little memorial meal as well, and raise a... raise a glass to Shirley. And then I sat and had a bit of lunch with Barney and had a little weep and now I'm about to continue on with my day, so I guess this is going to be the last of these recordings because I... I had decided that I was going to go up until the anniversary so that... so that it had been a year, and that's what I've done... so, yeah... so I guess this is the last one.

*

Everyone tells you not to make any major decisions while you're grieving, which I can see the logic of, but there is a fundamental problem with that advice. One thing I've learned is that your grief never leaves you – it just (hopefully) becomes easier to manage as your life expands around it and you begin to embrace a new normal – but if that's the case, at what point in that grief process does it become acceptable (or even advisable) to start making those big decisions?

My first thought after Shirley had gone was that I wanted to get a memorial tattoo. I've never had a tattoo before, so you might think this was a strange first thought to have, but it will make more sense when I tell you that between the break-up of my previous marriage and the point that Shirley and I got back together, I had a short period as a single parent to my (then) teenage son, and during that time we made a pact that if anything should happen to either one of us, the other would get a tattoo in their memory. So you can see how the idea would pop into my mind so readily.

Back in chapter twenty-nine, I spoke about the idea of a 'touchstone.' Well, in many ways, a tattoo is the ultimate touchstone – a permanent reminder I can't forget to put on or carry with me, nor can it be lost or stolen. It is a part of me, etched into my skin, just as Shirley herself is a part of me, etched into my heart and soul.

I wish I could say that Shirley would be proud of me for having it done, but she really didn't like them. I can hear her voice now, saying: "What have you been drawing on yourself for?" But although it has everything to do with our mutual love and affection, this is something just for me, a way of keeping her memory close and carrying her with me always, so I'm sure she would appreciate the symbolism and forgive me.

The strange thing is, since having it done (it didn't hurt, by the way – that's the first thing everybody asks) I have felt much more peaceful, much more attuned to my loss – as though the physical act of being 'inked' answered some need deep within me.

I think the truth is that when we are grieving so profoundly, we often feel as though everything is out of our control, that there is nothing we can do to alleviate that pain. Yet the tattoo has allowed me to take back a little control. It was a positive action I could take, something I could do to reaffirm my ongoing love for Shirley; a highly visible statement to the world.

And I can't tell you how much better I feel for having done it.

Chapter Fifty-Three
Looking forward

A good friend once asked me if, since Shirley's death, I found myself living in the past – and my reply was that no, I didn't, because to look back at what I had lost was too painful.

So somehow, I need to focus on the future… a future that, of course, no longer contains my love; no longer contains the hopes, the plans, the dreams that we had for our future together –and which now I must face alone.

I have had a great deal of help and support over this first year of bereavement, and much advice on strategies for going forward; from professionals in the field, from caring friends and close family, and from within the pages of the books I have read. But as I know only too well, what it really comes down to is discovering what works for you, and that will take as long as it takes. There is no deadline.

Mary-Frances O'Connell[22] makes a distinction between grieving (the process that you are going through) and grief (the emotional state that is triggered by any number of things – sometimes consciously, sometimes not – and which turns you into mush), the difference being that grieving is a lifelong state, while the effects of grief will lessen over time – and I find this a useful way to look at it.

It remains true, however, that in ways too numerous to mention, my own life ended in the early hours of that Easter Monday too, and that, I have come to accept, is at the heart of the state of grieving that she talks about.

Looking back, I see those first few months like being in a strait jacket – I was so constricted by my grief that I found it hard to function at all – yet as the year progressed I found ways to loosen the bonds a little, though every now and then grief would yank on the straps once more, often when I least expected it, and it would feel like I was back at square one.

But I wasn't.

I remain in the jacket, but it has gradually become more flexible and a little easier to move around in. Goodness knows how long it will take to shed it entirely, if indeed I ever do, but for now, on an objective level at least, I can see that there has been progress.

Losing a loved one changes you… you are no longer the person you were, but are part of the grieving community, a community that will ultimately encompass everyone on the planet. Loss, or the prospect of loss, is the one thing that we all have in common, death being an inescapable part of what it means to be human – the price we pay for life.

And grief is the cost of loving.

Yet bereavement by suicide puts you into a much more exclusive club. Clinicians refer to it as 'traumatic grieving' – a label that cuts both ways, for not only did your loved one die under traumatic circumstances, but their death also has a heart-rendingly traumatic effect on those around them. And that is something that can only really be understood by those who have been affected by it.

So my advice is to seek out those who are themselves grieving a loss by suicide – they have become your tribe, whether you like it or not. Speak with them, listen to them, weep with them – even, on occasion, laugh with them. Share your grief with those who understand, and life *will* become easier. It is a long, hard road, and we have no choice but to take it... one painful step at a time.

A simple online search will give you organisations who can help. In my case, it was Dorset Open Door[10] who fulfilled this role, and I cannot praise them enough. But organisations such as SOBS (Survivors of Bereavement by Suicide)[29] are nationwide and will put you in touch with others who have experienced a loss similar to your own. And never forget Samaritans[11]... always there at the end of a phone (116 123 in the UK) when your grief feels too much to bear.

So here I am, now firmly into my second year of bereavement, but where do I feel I am in relation to my 'grief journey'? Here are a handful of examples, most of which I have already alluded to through the pages of this book:

- I am still constantly affected by triggers of all kinds, but those attacks are no longer as extreme as they once were – often just a catch in my throat or a tear in my eye (though tears still flow freely on occasion) – and that is a huge improvement. However, I still have days which are completely awful, days when I find myself spiralling downwards unable to see how I will ever pull myself out. Yet somehow I do, and that at least gives me something to latch on to.

- Although I continue to have major issues with motivation, and enthusiasm for pretty much anything still eludes me, my ability to concentrate has improved immeasurably, almost back to previous levels, so that again is a major step forward.

- I have completed another course of therapy (this time a six-week course provided by the NHS, six weeks being the maximum they are currently prepared to fund) which proved to be much more probing and challenging than the counselling I had previously, and which regularly reduced me to pulp, but which in retrospect has been an extremely positive experience. As previously stated, I'm up for any help I can get, and will continue with that attitude for as long as it takes.

- I have also begun to realise that contrary to what I have believed throughout this last year, there have been – and continue to be – moments in which I have found pleasure, most notably through the antics of my little dog, when I have savoured a particularly delicious meal, or when I look down at my memorial tattoo. But the full-blown experience of joy continued to elude me, until I finally looked down into the face of my newborn grandson and wept, for the first time since Shirley died, with true, unadulterated joy.

- So now I find myself able to look tentatively forward to some kind of future – rather than just existing in a miserable and seemingly interminable present – but am still unclear as to what that future might look like. Counselling has been a godsend, and has helped me not only find ways of moving forward (not moving *on*, but moving *forward*, an important distinction) but also of dealing with the feelings of guilt that have plagued every moment of this last year. And that has been no mean feat. That is not to say that those feelings have disappeared, but that most days I am able to hold them at a manageable level.
What *is* true, is that I am no longer the person that I was, nor will ever be again.

- When it comes to my Christian faith however, that's still a work in progress. When Shirley died, it was as if a huge chasm had opened between myself and God. I could still see the other side – just about – but felt so far removed from it that it might as well not have been there. Yet as the months passed, I came to realise that there *were* still threads that connected me, and that slowly those threads have been pulling me back, gradually closing the chasm like sutures bringing together the two sides of a wound – which I guess is exactly what it is.

I recently attended a retreat at Lee Abbey[30] specifically concerned with navigating grief. I was a little anxious about the whole venture, knowing that it would be an emotional time, but all my attempts to reach out for help, all the courses and counselling and therapy, had up to this point been secular, and I felt the need for a Christian perspective. The place itself was beautiful, the people (both on the course and within the community) lovely, and the food fabulous, so any worries that I might have had about my time there were instantly dispelled. The two women who ran the course – both of whom had lost sons due to freak accidents so knew a thing or two about grief – were so kind, thoughtful and caring that I could not have asked for better. The whole experience turned out to be everything that I had hoped it would be, and more significantly gave me the spiritual boost that I so sorely needed.
One of the activities we were given was a creative writing exercise to write a lament based around one of the Old Testament Psalms, a task that I found particularly helpful, and I include it at the end of this chapter.
There's still a way to go, but things are improving, and I thank God for that. Like I say, a work in progress.

- And dreams? Well, I still have them, and they are still vivid and vibrant, though not all feature Shirley, which I guess you would expect. But the ones that do remain lovely to wake from, and continue to give me that warm glow of having been in her presence. A little while ago I dreamed that I met up with her at a music gig, and I was telling her what a good boy Barney had been, and how proud she would have been of him. Then only last night I dreamed that we were slow dancing together at a Science Fiction convention. The band played softly in the background, and we were lost in the moment, entranced by the sheer joy of holding each other close. Precious dreams indeed.

- Perhaps most importantly of all, though – as this book shows – is that I have reached a point where I can finally speak about Shirley's suicide, and I apologise again to all those who feel they were misled back in the beginning. Such was never my intention, and I hope that having read this book, you can understand why things unfolded as they did. I have profound admiration for those who talk bravely and openly about their loved one's suicide. I simply couldn't do it. Until now.

Have I reached a greater understanding as to why people feel they have no option but to take their lives? Certainly. I can understand, I can sympathise – even empathise to a certain degree – but I cannot *know* what it feels like to reach that crisis point, though there are far too many who do. Every day. That is the tragedy, and that is why it is important to talk about it – to raise awareness of just how heartbreakingly common it is, and how many lives are destroyed because of it.

In conclusion, if I have learned anything over this last year, it is that striving for answers and beating yourself up over what might have been is a fruitless exercise. It is inevitable, and guilt may run through us like the lettering in a stick of rock, but going round and round in circles is ultimately futile. Nothing will change what happened, or the new and unwanted reality in which we find ourselves. We cannot go back to make things right, to make things turn out differently, no matter how much we may yearn to do so. Somehow, we need to find a way to be kinder to ourselves; to forgive ourselves for what we may or may not have done in the run-up to our loved one's death; and to carry our loved one in our hearts as we set out upon the difficult road ahead. No one says that any of that is going to be easy, but I believe with all my heart that it is doable – if we give ourselves the time, and the space, to grieve.

For the terrible truth is that grief is an alien landscape, peppered with things that were once familiar, that once had a meaning, but which now are hardly recognisable. Like any traveller in a foreign land, you cast about for anything that might make sense to you, anything on which you can hang your current reality, anything that might explain where you are and what you should do next. There are guidebooks aplenty, but they all relate to someone else's experience, not yours – though you may find certain passages and descriptions that resonate.

Most days, finding a path through will seem impossible. But one day you will look back and realise that a year has passed, and you have no idea how you got to this point, but somehow you have. And that's a real positive.

One foot in front of the other, my friends.

It's all that we can do.

Lament
Inspired by Psalm 22

In my darkness, Lord, I flail and stumble, searching for your closeness, for the comfort of your nearness that has supported and nourished me for so long, yet is no more.

Have you abandoned me. Lord? Have you withdrawn your presence, leaving me alone and bereft?

A chasm has appeared within the darkness, separating you from me. It is a rift that I cannot close, a wound that I cannot suture.

Yet somehow, Lord, I know that you are there; there in the darkness; there above the chasm; there deep within this wound. I cannot feel you, yet I know and trust that you are there.

Let your light shine in my darkness, Lord. Illuminate my path. Draw the raw edges of this terrible wound together.

And beyond all else, take my hand and let me feel once more the joy of your presence.

For yours are the heavens and the earth, and all that therein is, including the darkness that envelops me.

Lost and alone I may be, but I know that your love encompasses me too, and that in time you will lift the veil that covers my eyes so that I may see once more the path that you have set before me.

The path that will lead me home

Kevin Burke

Lee Abbey, November 2024

References and links

1. https://www.woodlandtrust.org.uk
2. https://kbwillson.blogspot.com/2023/08/and-darkness-covered-the-face-of-the-earth.html?m=1
3. https://www.fairportconvention.com
4. Coles, Rev Richard (2021) *The Madness of Grief* Weidenfeld & Nicolson p.130
5. Shakespeare, *Macbeth* Act 5, Scene 5, lines 17-28
6. Lewis, C.S. (1961) *A Grief Observed* Faber & Faber
7. Kubler-Ross, E. (1969) *On Death and Dying* Macmillan
8. Shakespeare, *Hamlet* Act 1 Scene 5, lines 165-166
9. St Matthew's Gospel, chapter 22, verse 30. *King James Bible*
10. https//www.dorsethealthcare.nhs.uk/patients-and-visitors/our-services-hospitals/mental-health/dorset-open-door
11. https://www.facingthefuturegroups.org
12. https://www.samaritans.org
13. Mikhalkova, Elena "The Room of Ancient Keys" *FB page: Midwives of the Soul* 24/4/20

14. Safka, Melanie "Look what they've done to my song, ma" *Candles in the Rain* (1970) Buddha
15. Anderson, Jamie Originally posted on www.allmylooseends.com
16. Shakespeare, *The Tempest* Act 4, Scene 1, lines 156-158
17. Mitchell, Joni, "Big Yellow Taxi" *Ladies of the Canyon* (1970) Reprise
18. https://www.youtube.com/watch?v=eEsxo01gVks&t=14s
19. www.sararianbooks.com
20. Lynch, Paul "Is Prophet Song a mirror of modern-day fascism" *Talk to Al Jazeera* 21/1/24
21. Acts of the Apostles chapter 2, verse 17 *New International Version*
22. O'Connor, Mary-Frances (2022) *The Grieving Brain* Harper Collins
23. https://www.suicideandco.org
24. Thomas, R.S. (1964) "In Church" *The Bread of Truth* Hart-Davis
25. Burns, Robert (1786) "To a Mouse, on Turning Her Up in Her Nest with the Plough" *The Kilmarnock Volume* Wilson
26. https://www.steps2wellbeing.co.uk
27. Ashworth, Donna (2022) "Peace at Last" *Loss* Black and White Publishing
28. Foster, Jeff (2016) *The Way of Rest* Sounds True Adult
29. www.uk-sobs.org.uk
30. https//leeabbeydevon.org.uk

Acknowledgments

I made the decision early on that I wouldn't refer to anyone other than myself, Shirley, and Barney by name, but there are many friends and family, neighbours and colleagues who are mentioned throughout in an anonymous capacity, and many more who are not, yet without whom I wouldn't have made it this far, much less be publishing this book.

All I can say is that you know who you are, and I am so, so grateful to each and every one of you.

About the Author

Kevin Burke is a British actor/author/entertainer currently living beside the sea in Dorset. After studying Theology and English at St. John's College Durham, he went on to spend his working life in the fields of theatre and performance, where he has worked as an actor, director, fight director, playwright, magician, jester, fire-eater, juggler, and stilt walker, to name but a few. He has taught performing arts at both BTEC and HND level, as well as running numerous drama and circus skills workshops around the country.

He also writes speculative fiction under the pen name KB Willson.

More information about Kevin and his work can be found at

www.kevinburke.co.uk

www.kbwillson.com

https://kbwillson.blogspot.com

Printed in Great Britain
by Amazon